The Secret Gospel

THE LAUGHING MAN SERIES

Our era is marked by the urgent need for, but also the possibility of, conscious cooperation between all traditions and individuals. As the contemporary Adept Da Free John has observed: "It is no longer appropriate or even possible for individuals, cultures, or nations to justify absolute independence from other individuals, cultures, or nations—and it is no longer appropriate or possible to grant absolute or ultimately superior status to any historical Revelation, belief system, or conception of how things work. The entire Great Tradition must be accepted as our common inheritance. We need not (as a method for achieving Realization or Enlightenment) base our lives on the affirmation of belief in the Great Tradition (in part or as a whole) as Revelation, but we must overcome the provincialism of our minds (and, ultimately, the provincialism that is mind itself)."

What Master Da Free John calls "the Great Tradition" is the totality of traditions reflecting all aspects of the great school of human life. It represents our common human heritage and therefore it is of immediate significance to everyone.

The Dawn Horse Press is dedicated to the publication, in The Laughing Man Series, of works of authentic philosophical, religious, and spiritual genius from the Great Tradition in order to foster the spirit of mutual understanding and cooperation between people and, beyond that, to help establish a genuine spiritual culture of respect, service, love, self-transcendence, and ultimate God-Realization.

This volume is part of The Laughing Man Series, published by The Dawn Horse Press in cooperation with the Editorial Department of The Johannine Daist Communion.

The Secret Gospel

The Discovery and Interpretation of the Secret Gospel According to Mark

Morton Smith

The Dawn Horse Press
Clearlake, California

The photographs on pages 33, 35, 36 (top), and 37 are reprinted with permission from *Archaeology,* Vol. 13, No. 3, copyright 1960, Archaeological Institute of America.

First Dawn Horse Press edition published 1982.
Reprinted 1984.

ISBN: 0-913922-55-2
Library of Congress Catalog Card Number: 82-73215

FOR THE ONE
WHO KNOWS

Contents

Foreword

Whoever begins to investigate evidence concerning Jesus of Nazareth discovers the historians' dilemma: our earliest sources, the gospels, were written down at least a generation after his death, and intended less as historical biography than as confessions of faith. Yet from these slight beginnings, massive traditions have developed during nearly 2,000 years. Further, Jesus' role as founder of Christianity, the symbolic center of the faith, has given many the impression that they know intimately who this mysterious person was—or is.

The Secret Gospel offers new evidence to challenge such certainties. Was Jesus a magician? Did he initiate his closest followers into ecstatic visions of heaven, using hallucinatory technique, to share with them his experience of liberation from Jewish law? In *The Secret Gospel,* Professor Morton Smith of Columbia University presents new evidence—his own discovery of a fragment of a secret, expanded version of the Gospel of Mark—that, he explains, led him to these surprising conclusions.

The claim that Jesus taught secretly, startling at first, finds support even within the New Testament itself. According to Mark 4:10, Jesus confides to his disciples, "To you has been given the secret of the Kingdom of God, but for those outside everything is in parables; so that they may indeed see but not perceive, and may indeed hear but not understand; lest they should turn again, and be forgiven." The apostle Paul, too, writes to Christians in Corinth that, when he preached there, he "decided to acknowledge nothing, among you, except Jesus Christ . . . crucified. Yet," Paul continues, "among the mature [or: initiated] we do impart wisdom . . . we impart a secret and hidden wisdom of God." Historical evidence, as Professor Smith shows, makes this plausible. Rabbinic circles, such as those in which Paul received his education, developed esoteric teachings and practices, which they carefully hid from outsiders.

Recent archaeological finds have added new evidence. The Dead Sea Scrolls, discovered in 1945, disclosed the writings of the Essene Jewish community, which bound its members with oaths of secrecy. Even more remarkable are the discoveries at Nag Hammadi in Upper Egypt, where an Arab peasant accidentally unearthed a library of ancient texts, including several gospels, and a collection of Christian revelations. Among them was found the esoteric Gospel of Thomas, which opens with the words, "These are the *secret* words that the Living Jesus spoke . . ."

We have long known that such texts circulated widely in Christian communities in the late first and early second centuries. Around 160 A.D., however, Irenaeus, orthodox bishop of Lyons, denounced all such writings as heresy:

"(The heretics) boast that they possess more gospels than there really are . . . (but) they really have no gospel which is not full of blasphemy."

Only four gospels, Irenaeus insisted, give authentic accounts of Jesus—the gospels of the New Testament. He offers two kinds of "proof" for his statement. First, he appeals to the natural symmetry of the number; as there are four corners of the universe, and four primary winds, so, he concludes, there can be only four gospels. Second, Irenaeus says that only these four were written by

Jesus' own followers (Matthew and John) or their own disciples (Mark and Luke). Few Biblical scholars today accept the traditional view that the disciples themselves wrote those gospels. Many of the recently discovered texts also are attributed to disciples (for example, the gospels of Thomas, Mary, and Philip); in either case, such claims are historically unprovable.

Professor Smith's discovery, then, contributes. to current discussion—and sharp debate—on the sources of early Christian tradition. In *The Secret Gospel* he communicates the excitement of his meticulous detective work: Professor Smith is that rarity among scholars, an excellent writer. Among his colleagues he is well known and respected for the range and precision of his learning; his many other books include *The Ancient History of Western Civilization,* written with Professor Elias Bickerman; *Palestinian Parties and Politics that Shaped the Old Testament,* and *The Ancient Greeks.* In 1980, The Society of Biblical Literative honored Professor Smith by awarding him the Ralph Marcus Award for Scholarship Supplementary to New Testament Studies. Together with *The Secret Gospel* he published, through Harvard University Press, a much fuller and more technical account of the discovery, addressed to other specialists.

While his scholarly credentials are impeccable, Professor Smith's theory—as he himself anticipated—has proven to be explosively controversial. Some critics, outraged at the view of Jesus he presents, have written potential attacks. Others, startled by his conclusions, are now reexamining the evidence, questioning, for example, the authenticity of *The Secret Gospel,* and debating his interpretation of its meaning. Among scholars, the debates his research has initiated are just beginning; no doubt they will continue for decades. Meanwhile, *The Secret Gospel* invites a wide community of readers to share in the challenge of his discovery, and to evaluate for themselves the provocative—and fundamental—questions it raises.

Elaine H. Pagels
author, *The Gnostic Gospels*

Preface

This book is the story of a series of discoveries—not only the discovery of a manuscript (which I found in 1958 at the Monastery of Mar Saba in the Judean desert), but also the events that led to the finding and the steps by which, after I had the text, I gradually discovered its significance for the history of the life of Jesus, the course of early Christianity, and the interpretation of the New Testament. The whole story spans more than thirty years, from 1941 to the present. I am shocked to find how much of it I have already forgotten. No doubt if the past, like a motion picture, could be replayed, I should also be shocked to find how much of the story I have already invented. Memory is perhaps more fallacious than forgetfulness. But here, at least, is what I think I remember.

For conversations I have followed the example of Thucydides and have made people say what I remember they did say in substance, using the words I think they might have used. Quotation marks indicate only this, when they stand in conversations; elsewhere they have their normal meanings. The translations, throughout, are my own, except when otherwise noted. In translating the Scriptures I have tried to render as accurately as possible their irregularities in the use of tenses and other grammatical details.

M.S.

1

The Preparation

"After the Christmas season," Father Kyriakos said to me, "I shall go down to Mar Saba for a few days. You must come, too."

That was in 1941, when I was twenty-six. I had gone out to Jerusalem on a traveling fellowship from Harvard Divinity School, had got stuck there when the Mediterranean was closed by the war, and had started work for a doctorate in philosophy at the Hebrew University and found myself an apartment in the old city. By good luck I found it in a Greek hostel beside the Church of the Holy Sepulchre. The hostel was a former monastery and Father Kyriakos lived there as its superior. He was really Archimandrite Kyriakos Spyridonides, Custodian of the Holy Sepulchre, one of the highest dignitaries of the Greek Orthodox Patriarchate of Jerusalem, but I knew him first as a pleasant old gentleman who drove a good bargain for the apartment, but then went out of his way to help me deal with the innumerable problems of life in a new and strange society.

Thanks to him I saw much of the Holy Sepulchre and fell in love with it and with the Greek Orthodox services. The great cathedral was then undergoing extensive repairs for earthquake damages. It was a tangle of struts and trestles, of mysterious shadows, tiny passageways, and unexpected enormous spaces, of bare wood and iron supports, of gilded carvings and magnificent marble. Through this fantastic structure passed the long lines of priests and monks in their black robes and glittering vestments, while from above came the clang and thunder of the huge Russian bells. At the beginning of the mass, with the majestic opening of the great doors of the golden altar screen, the unspeakable solemnity of the procedure, I understood what the northern barbarians must have felt when they were permitted to enter Byzantium.

What most of all delighted me was the music. From the Protestant tradition, where church music has a uniform tone of respectable reverence and the organ is regularly used to cover the inadequacy of the performers, I had no idea of what could be done with unaccompanied choirs, nor of the variety and vivacity of the music for the Greek monastic services, which can go from gaiety to grandeur, from passion to awe, with unmatched lightness and power. Father Kyriakos gave me permission to stand in the choir so that I could see the texts as they were sung. (There was little written music; most of the tunes were traditional.) Soon I was memorizing words and tunes, probably to the horror of my neighbors. It may not have been unadulterated altruism that prompted the invitation to go to Mar Saba.

Whatever the motive, I was delighted by the invitation. I had often heard of Mar Saba. With St. Catherine's on Mt. Sinai, it was one of the two great desert monasteries of the Orthodox Church, monasteries in which the Byzantine order of services and way of life were still preserved. St. Saba—in Arabic, Mar Saba—its founder, had lived in the fifth century, roughly a thousand five hundred years ago, and ever since, with brief interruptions, there had been some sort of monastic life at the site.[1]

---

1. Unfortunately, the only good history of the monastery is in Greek: J. Phokylides, *He hiera Laura Saba tou hegiasmenou*, Alexandria, 1927. Phokylides has refuted the report of Sophronius (repeated by Khitrowo, Erhard, Strzygowski, and others) that the site was abandoned from 1450 to 1540; see *Laura*, pp. 506–521.

We set out early one morning with the old man who every week took the monastery its food—its only connection with the modern world. Father Kyriakos, who did a good deal of riding, went ahead on his horse; I had a donkey and an Arab boy to drive him; the man followed, driving the other donkeys with the luggage. It was a journey into the middle ages.

The monastery lies in the desert, roughly a dozen miles southeast of Jerusalem. In those days the trail to it lay along the wadi (canyon) that runs from Jerusalem down to the Dead Sea. For a short way there were houses and a little cultivation along the edge of the stream, but then the desert closed in—rocks and gravel and silence except for the crunch of the animals' footsteps. After we had ridden for an hour or so we came suddenly, around a corner of rock, on an Arab butchering a camel. The beast was already dead and on its back, with its great legs sticking into the air at odd angles, and the butcher was at work on it with an old saber. He was naked from the waist up and had blood all over him. The sunlight, the red blood, the brown body, the magenta and purple of the skinned legs and carcass, the orange and gray rocks, the black silhouette of that saber swinging in the air, I shall never forget. I remember also the sweat (it glittered) and the flies. We exchanged greetings and rode on. Later we passed some caves. The women who lived in them came out to look at us and waved and shouted. Then more desert. Finally, a little after noon, we came over a rise and saw the monastery lying below us—a strong, medieval tower dominating two curtain walls that closed off a stretch of the wadi's rim and then plunged down it. The trail zigzagged past the tower and down to a narrow, fortified gate in the wall below.

There was no radio at Mar Saba. The existence of the outside world was not denied; it was not mentioned. Father Kyriakos arranged for me to stay on after his departure, and I must have spent almost two months there, two months of absolute peace in a world of which the only concern was the daily round of work and worship.

Worship began at midnight and went on without interruption until about six in the morning. This was on ordinary days; on festivals it lasted longer. After the service there was bread and coffee. The meal of the day was at noon, and about one-thirty the afternoon service began. It went on for a couple of hours; then there was a brief intermission; about five o'clock came half an hour of evening prayers; after that one slept until midnight. Between the services there was silence—the silence of the desert, no voices, no sounds of animals, not even wind in the trees.

In their free moments the monks showed me around the monastery and also took me to visit some of the caves that lined the walls of the wadi on both sides up and down stream. Many of the caves had formerly been the homes of hermits, and in some one could still see the remains of old paintings and inscriptions. In a few of them, I was told, fragments of manuscripts had been found. Moreover, the caves were excellent hiding places. Many had mouths that only an expert climber could reach, and often the mouths were so small as to be almost unnoticeable from the floor of the wadi. In such caves the monks had hidden when the monastery was sacked in times of war or persecution. There was a story, too, that on one occasion the monk in charge of the monastery's treasures, fearing an attack by the bedouin, had hidden a lot of the finest manuscripts in a cave known only to himself and his assistant. The attack came, both of them were killed, and the manuscripts were never recovered. The story sounds like romance; but this same wadi runs by Qumran where the spectacular finds came from a Jewish "monastery." Its inmates hid their manuscripts in neighboring caves when a Roman attack was impending. The attack destroyed the community (four hundred years before Mar Saba was founded) and the manuscripts remained in the caves until their recent discovery. Exploration of other wadis along the edge of the Dead Sea and the Jordan valley has shown that the caves in them have been used for dwellings and places of refuge, off and on, since neolithic times.

In such caves the monastery had begun. Many of the cells were still caves with only a facing built across the front of them. The whole structure clung to the cliff face like a gigantic swallow's nest, with terrace above terrace yielding, at most, a garden plot for cultivation, often a mere path to another terrace. The new church had been built in the nineteenth century on monumental piers that rose from far down in the wadi, but earlier the church, too, had been in one of the largest caves, where services were still sometimes held. Here were many of the most beautiful icons, and here, I was told, had occurred the great fire, sometime in the eighteenth century, when many of the finest icons, manuscripts, and vestments, stored in the inner windings of the cave, were destroyed. Most of the remaining manuscripts had been carried off to Jerusalem in the late nineteenth century, at the order of the Patriarch, but there were still a few stored in the great tower, and there was a good library of old editions of the Church fathers in a room over the porch of the new church.

I was shown the two libraries, as I was the other sights of the monastery, but at the time I paid them little attention. My main interest was in the services, which gave me a new understanding of worship as a means of disorientation. The six hours in darkness with which the day began were not long—they were eternal. The service was not moving toward its end, it was simply going on, as it had from eternity and would forever. As one ceased to be in time, one ceased also to be in a definite space. In the enormous church, lit only by the flames of scattered sanctuary lights and candles, there were no visible walls, floor, or ceiling. The few small flames far above, like stars, burned again on the polished marble of the nave, as if other stars were an equal distance below. Or were those tiny fires, far down beneath, the earth? The painted walls reflected the dim light as if it came from a remote distance, and in the vast, vaguely luminous space thus created the huge black frescoes of the saints and monks of old stood like solid presences all around, the great figures of the eternal and universal Church, present in this realm among the stars, above space and time, the unchanging kingdom of the heavens, where the eternal service was offered to eternal God.

The words of this worship, too—the enormous hymns of the Greek monastic offices—were unmistakably hypnotic, interminably ringing the changes on a relatively small number of brilliant, ex-aggerated metaphors, dazzling the mind and destroying its sense of reality. I knew what was happening, but I relaxed and enjoyed it. Yet at the same time I somehow came to realize that I did not want to stay. For the monks, it was truth, for me it was poetry; their practice was based on faith, mine on a willing suspension of dis-belief. When Father Kyriakos came down again, early in Lent, I was ready to return to Jerusalem, went back with him, and re-sumed my work at the university.

When I began this chapter my conscious intention was merely to explain how I happened to go back to Mar Saba, years later, and find the manuscript. Also I wanted the pleasure of recalling this strange and beautiful experience, and the advantage of be-ginning my book with this picturesque material. But just now, while writing, I see this story has introduced one of the important themes of the book. For what I really discovered in this first visit to Mar Saba was the inner purpose of the Orthodox liturgy: to make the worshipers on earth participants in the perpetual worship of heaven. And this discovery, I now realize, provided one of the key ideas by which I was later enabled to explain the Gospel ma-terial in the manuscript. Is this a coincidence? Or has the mystical tradition of Greek monasticism, which shaped the hymns and suggested my experience, preserved and developed the primitive

Christian tradition that lay behind the Gospel? Or have I imposed on the Gospel my understanding of the Orthodox rites?

Another element in my experience at Mar Saba now also seems significant. I became aware of a fundamental difference between my attitude toward the service and that of the monks. For me, at that time, the liturgy was primarily a means for the experience of beauty, and thus a means of revelation, since beauty was of God. For the monks, the liturgy was just what its Greek name said— *leitourgia* means "service"—and this service was primarily a duty. Certain words had to be said, certain actions, to be performed. Whether or not the result was beautiful was, at best, a secondary concern. The mere performance was both essential and effective. This attitude is basically magical. For example, it explains the magical gems of the ancient world, on which spells and figures are often scribbled with no regard at all for appearance, but with an iron determination to get the necessary words and patterns, some- how or other, onto the stone. During my visit I simply thought the monks' attitude curious, but I now suppose it helped to shape my understanding of the religious mind and subsequently, without my recalling it, to explain the new Gospel text.

Another important element of the later pattern appeared during my stay in Jerusalem. I had, by chance, met Professor Gershom Scholem whose great book, *Major Trends in Jewish Mysticism*, was just then being prepared for publication. He asked me to read over the English translation. I was fascinated by what I found, and most of all by the account of the *hekalot* books. *Hekal* (plural, *hekalot*) means "hall" or "palace," but in late antiquity it came to be used of the heavens, the palace of the great King. At that time some Jews had developed a technique of self-hypnosis which gave them the experience of ascending into the heavens and sitting on the throne of God. The technique consisted mainly in the recita- tion of long rhythmical prayers and hymns and lists of angels with terrific, resonant names, like Seganzagael. The texts often had prose

comments telling how great rabbis had used the formulae and
what to expect when using it, and so on. Texts and comments
circulated in a number of collections called the *hekalot* books. Unfortunately, they didn't work, but they interested me because the
experiences they described were so much like those I had glimpsed
in the monastery. And they came, in the main, from late antiquity
and the early middle ages, roughly from the same period and the
same area as the monastic tradition. Was there any connection
between them?

I remember, too, that I did some reading about the Baal Shem,
the legendary founder of Hasidism. Scholem has called attention
to a letter the Baal Shem wrote about 1752 to R. Gershon of Kuty,
telling "of a visionary 'ascent of the soul' to heaven which he experienced in September 1746. Such experiences, as he has testified
himself, came to him not infrequently, and he was able to induce
them by his own volition."[2] Did I come across the Baal Shem's
letter at that time, or did other stories of his ascents to heaven get
into my memory and lie dormant? I don't remember.

For almost seventeen years all such experiences went unused. At
the Hebrew University, for three years, I worked on the relations
of the Gospels to the earliest rabbinic literature, from which magic
and mysticism have almost wholly been weeded out. Just as I
finished my thesis[3] the Mediterranean was reopened for American
convoys. I went home on the first one I could get and soon found
myself back at Harvard, working for a second doctoral degree, this
time in theology. Under the influence of Professor Werner Jaeger,
an outstanding classical and patristic scholar, I became interested
in Greek manuscripts and manuscript hunting. But other fields
of research also attracted me and a great deal of my time went into
teaching, first at Brown University, then at Drew, finally at Co-

---

2. Scholem, *The Messianic Idea in Judaism,* New York, 1971, p. 182.

3. *Maqbilot ben haBesorot le Sifrut haTannd'im,* Jerusalem, 1948; English
translation, revised, *Tannaitic Parallels to the Gospels,* Philadelphia, 1951, reprinted 1968 (*Journal of Biblical Literature Monograph Series* VI).

lumbia. By the spring of 1958 I was ready for a rest and remembered the tranquillity of Mar Saba.

During all this time I had corresponded with Father Kyriakos and after 1948, when the division of Palestine flooded the Patriarchate with destitute Orthodox refugees, I had taken an active part in organizing an "American Friends" group that raised some money for their relief. Consequently the new Patriarch, His Beatitude Benedict, graciously gave me permission to spend three weeks at Mar Saba, study the manuscripts there, and publish my findings. For that permission, this book is an inadequate expression of thanks. Little did I know that one find of the summer would push all my other plans into abeyance for half a dozen years.

2

The Discovery

Never revisit a place that fascinated you when you were young —you discover not only its changes, but your own. Much at Jerusalem, of course, was the same. Father Kyriakos was genial and wise as ever. Many of my other friends in the Patriarchate seemed almost unchanged. But as I whizzed out to Mar Saba by taxi (twenty minutes from the city along the new military road) I foresaw what was coming.

Electricity had been introduced, and not even the magic of the Byzantine liturgy can survive direct illumination. Perhaps that was just as well; it enabled me to blame the lighting for my own failure to respond at forty-three as I had at twenty-six. Six hours of a service to which one is not responding are a bit too much, but as a guest of the Patriarch I was under no obligation to attend. I soon made my supposed scholarly labors an excuse for spending most of my time in my cell, enjoying the solitude and the silence for which the monastery had been founded. My old friend, Archimandrite Seraphim, was now in charge and saw to it that the traditional order was maintained. Thus one tranquil, silent day followed another as I devoted myself to locating, reading, and cataloguing the manuscripts.

Every morning except Sunday, after the services, a monk would climb with me the long stairways that led to the old tower—they must have amounted to a dozen or fifteen stories—and sit by patiently while I went through volume after volume of the books and manuscripts piled every which way on the floor and in the bookcases that lined the side walls of the topmost room. I first cleared one shelf of a bookcase and then began lining up there the printed books I had inspected. When a volume turned out to contain manuscript material, I set it aside. When I had found three or four manuscripts we called it a day. The room was locked and I took the manuscripts down to my cell for study. Next morning I returned them, worked through another pile or two of volumes, found another few manuscripts, and so continued. Little by little the chaos of old books was reduced to order, and, as the line of printed texts grew along one side of the room, a much smaller line of catalogued manuscripts began to grow along the other.

I had not expected much from the Mar Saba manuscripts, since I knew that almost all of them had been carried off to Jerusalem in the past century and were listed in the catalogue of the Patriarchal library. But there was always the chance that something had been missed, or that other manuscripts had been brought in by monks coming from other monasteries. In any event it would be helpful to know what was in the library.[1] So I patiently listed manuscript copies of prayer books and hymns and sermons and lives of saints and anthologies from the Church fathers and so on —the proper and predictable reading of a monastic community.

Many of the printed books contained extensive handwritten passages. Binders' pages at front and back, blank pages between chapters, even margins had been pressed into use. Evidently paper had been in short supply at Mar Saba during the seventeenth, eighteenth, and nineteenth centuries, from which almost all of these copies came.

1. The complete list of my findings, translated and edited by Archimandrite Constantine Michaelides, was published in the periodical of the Patriarchate, *Nea Sion*, under the title, "Hellenika Cheirographa en tei Monei tou Hagiou Sabba," 52(1960)110ff and 245ff.

I also found that much older manuscript material had been used for bookbinding. Two folia of a fifteenth-century manuscript of Sophocles, for instance, had been used as end papers for an eighteenth-century Venice edition of the evening and morning prayers.[2] Where bindings were torn, I sometimes caught glimpses of yet older writing underneath them. Evidently at some time in the past the monks had a lot of odd pages from medieval manuscripts and glued them together to make cardboard for binding more recent works. I guessed that this happened after the great fire in the eighteenth century. Books are hard to burn, so that fire must have left a lot of them charred on the outside and ready to fall apart, but with their central pages almost undamaged. This guess, though, did nothing to recover the lost texts. My permission to study the volumes did not include permission to take them apart. So I was gradually reconciling myself to my worst expectations and repeating every day that I should discover nothing of importance.

Then, one afternoon near the end of my stay, I found myself in my cell, staring incredulously at a text written in a tiny scrawl I had not even tried to read in the tower when I picked out the book containing it. But now that I came to puzzle it out, it began, "From the letters of the most holy Clement, the author of the *Stromateis*. To Theodore," and it went on to praise the recipient for having "shut up" the Carpocratians. The *Stromateis,* I knew, was a work by Clement of Alexandria, one of the earliest and most mysterious of the great fathers of the Church—early Christian writers of outstanding importance. I was reasonably sure that no letters of his had been preserved. So if this writing was what it claimed to be, I had a hitherto unknown text by a writer of major significance for early Church history. Besides, it would add something to our knowledge of the Carpocratians, one of the most scandalous of the "gnostic" sects, early and extreme variants of Christianity. Who

2. These pages I have described in "New Fragments of Scholia on Sophocles' Ajax," *Greek, Roman and Byzantine Studies* 3 (1960) 40ff.

Theodore was, I had no idea. I still don't. But Clement and the Carpocratians were more than enough for one day. I hastened to photograph the text and photographed it three times for good measure. Next came the question of identifying the book into the back of which it was written. The front cover and the title page were lost (most of the books in the tower library had lived hard lives), and there was nothing on the spine, but I could see that it was an edition of the letters of St. Ignatius of Antioch (another early Church father). The preface had been signed by the famous seventeenth-century Dutch scholar, Isaac Voss. Voss' work on Ignatius had been published several times, I knew, but it occurred to me that I could date the edition by photographing the first and last preserved pages and comparing them with complete volumes, so I took those. (The edition eventually turned out to be that of 1646.) Then the bell rang for vespers, and I went off, walking on air.

The next day brought other manuscripts and other problems. If I wanted to catalogue the library, I couldn't sit down and study one text in detail. And a library that had yielded one such text might yield another. The day after that, in fact, I came on an old binding so far gone to pieces that I could get out the "boards" around which the leather had been sewn. They had been made by gluing together pages of a fifteenth-century manuscript of "St. Macarius of Egypt"—a name used to disguise a collection of tracts by ancient Syrian heretics. I tried a little water on one corner, to see if the ink would run. It proved waterproof, so I was able, by soaking the pages, to separate them and recover almost a dozen, several of which turned out to contain fragments of texts unknown to the standard editions. With this my stay came to an end. I went back to Jerusalem, spent a few days with Father Kyriakos, and then crossed into Israel to visit my former teachers at the Hebrew University.

No sooner was I in Israel than I found a good photographer and left my films to be developed and printed. Photographing manuscripts is a tricky business, especially when the camera has to be held by hand, so I was anxious. By good luck all the shots turned out well (I had photographed half a dozen texts of the seventy-five I catalogued), and I was able to sit down and begin to study them.

I told Scholem about the letter of Clement and he pounced immediately on the mention of the Carpocratians. Carpocrates was said to have taught that sin was a means of salvation. Only by committing all possible actions could the soul satisfy the demands of the rulers of this world and so be permitted to go on to the heavens, its true home. A remotely similar theme was important in the writings of some seventeenth- and eighteenth-century Jewish heretics whom Scholem had been studying (Sabbatai Zevi and Jacob Frank), and years of experience in the Eranos circle had made him well aware of the importance of parallel phenomena for the history of religion, so he hoped for more information about Carpocrates.

Then I finished my transcription and translation. What I found threw poor Carpocrates, and even Clement, completely into the shade. The text read as follows (I have added the bracketed words to make the meaning clear.):

> From the letters of the most holy Clement, author of the *Stromateis.* To Theodore:
>
> You did well in silencing the unspeakable teachings of the Carpocratians. For these are the "wandering stars" referred to in the prophecy, who wander from the narrow road of the commandments into a boundless abyss of the carnal and bodily sins. For, priding themselves in knowledge, as they say, "of the deep [things] of Satan," they do not know that they are casting themselves away into "the nether world of the darkness" of falsity, and, boasting that they are free, they have become slaves of servile desires. Such [men] are to be opposed in all ways and altogether. For, even if they should say something

true, one who loves the truth should not, even so, agree with them. For not all true [things] are the truth, nor should that truth which [merely] seems true according to human opinions be preferred to the true truth, that according to the faith.

Now of the [things] they keep saying about the divinely inspired Gospel according to Mark, some are altogether falsifications, and others, even if they do contain some true [elements], nevertheless are not reported truly. For the true [things], being mixed with inventions, are falsified, so that, as the saying [goes], even the salt loses its savor.

[As for] Mark, then, during Peter's stay in Rome he wrote [an account of] the Lord's doings, not, however, declaring all [of them], nor yet hinting at the secret [ones], but selecting those he thought most useful for increasing the faith of those who were being instructed. But when Peter died as a martyr, Mark came over to Alexandria, bringing both his own notes and those of Peter, from which he transferred to his former book the things suitable to whatever makes for progress toward knowledge [*gnosis*]. [Thus] he composed a more spiritual Gospel for the use of those who were being perfected. Nevertheless, he yet did not divulge the things not to be uttered, nor did he write down the hierophantic teaching of the Lord, but to the stories already written he added yet others and, moreover, brought in certain sayings of which he knew the interpretation would, as a mystagogue, lead the hearers into the innermost sanctuary of that truth hidden by seven [veils]. Thus, in sum, he prearranged matters, neither grudgingly nor incautiously, in my opinion, and, dying, he left his composition to the church in Alexandria, where it even yet is most carefully guarded, being read only to those who are being initiated into the great mysteries.

But since the foul demons are always devising destruction for the race of men, Carpocrates, instructed by them and using

deceitful arts, so enslaved a certain presbyter of the church in
Alexandria that he got from him a copy of the secret Gospel,
which he both interpreted according to his blasphemous and
carnal doctrine and, moreover, polluted, mixing with the spot-
less and holy words utterly shameless lies. From this mixture
is drawn off the teaching of the Carpocratians.

To them, therefore, as I said above, one must never give
way, nor, when they put forward their falsifications, should
one concede that the secret Gospel is by Mark, but should even
deny it on oath. For, "Not all true [things] are to be said to all
men." For this [reason] the Wisdom of God, through
Solomon, advises, "Answer the fool from his folly," teaching
that the light of the truth should be hidden from those who
are mentally blind. Again it says, "From him who has not
shall be taken away," and, "Let the fool walk in darkness."
But we are "children of light," having been illuminated by
"the dayspring" of the Spirit of the Lord "from on high," and
"Where the Spirit of the Lord is," it says, "there is liberty,"
for "All things are pure to the pure."

To you, therefore, I shall not hesitate to answer the [ques-
tions] you have asked, refuting the falsifications by the very
words of the Gospel. For example, after "And they were in
the road going up to Jerusalem," and what follows, until
"After three days he shall arise," [the secret Gospel] brings
the following [material] word for word:

"And they come into Bethany, and a certain woman, whose
brother had died, was there. And, coming, she prostrated herself before Jesus and says to him, 'Son of David, have mercy
on me.' But the disciples rebuked her. And Jesus, being
angered, went off with her into the garden where the tomb
was, and straightway a great cry was heard from the tomb.
And going near Jesus rolled away the stone from the door of
the tomb. And straightway, going in where the youth was, he

stretched forth his hand and raised him, seizing his hand. But the youth, looking upon him, loved him and began to beseech him that he might be with him. And going out of the tomb they came into the house of the youth, for he was rich. And after six days Jesus told him what to do and in the evening the youth comes to him, wearing a linen cloth over [his] naked [body]. And he remained with him that night, for Jesus taught him the mystery of the kingdom of God. And thence, arising, he returned to the other side of the Jordan."

After these [words] follows the text, "And James and John come to him," and all that section. But "naked [man] with naked [man]" and the other things about which you wrote are not found.

And after the [words], "And he comes into Jericho," [the secret Gospel] adds only, "And the sister of the youth whom Jesus loved and his mother and Salome were there, and Jesus did not receive them." But the many other [things about] which you wrote both seem to be and are falsifications.

Now the true explanation and that which accords with the true philosophy . . .

Here the text broke off, in the middle of a page.

3

The Problems

Even before I finished transcribing the text, I began to think it was too good to be true. Here was new information about Jesus, a new miracle story, a quotation from a secret Gospel by St. Mark, and the information that Mark had written a second, secret Gospel, and that Clement's church, as well as the Carpocratians, had used it! If the letter was really by Clement I had a discovery of extraordinary importance. But if it was a fake of some sort and I rushed into print with an announcement of a "great discovery," I could make myself an internationally conspicuous fool. So I kept my mouth shut.

The schedule of my trip took me off to Istanbul. By the time I got there I was badly upset. Moments of wild excitement alternated with spells of profound pessimism and even resentment. The thing just couldn't be true; it was too important! Why had nobody else ever mentioned the secret Gospel of Mark, if there was one? And why did it have to be my luck to walk into this trap? I couldn't suppress it; I'd already told Scholem. —But then, why shouldn't it be genuine? The handwriting of the manuscript must be, roughly, of the eighteenth century. Who, at that time, in a Greek monastery dedicated to the devotional life, could have made up such a thing? What monk knew anything about Carpocrates? What motive could there possibly have been for the invention of such

a document? —But if it were genuine, then . . . ! And so off again
into excitement, and then back to depression.

The sheer physical labor of traveling around Turkey and Greece
and climbing over the ruins of ancient cities in the midsummer
sun gradually brought me back to normal. By the time I had
worked my way through Thrace and Macedonia and on to Athens
I was able to sit down calmly and assess the situation.

First of all, I must get expert opinions on the handwriting. The
history of handwriting is a highly specialized field. Experts can
often tell you where, sometimes even by whom, a manuscript was
written. They can usually date one within about fifty years. (Many
think they can do even better than this, but I am skeptical. I have
an old aunt whose handwriting hasn't changed perceptibly in the
past fifty years; a trained scribe's hand would be even less likely
to change.) Anyhow, expert opinions I had to have, and the fore-
most scholars in the world for the study of modern Greek manuscript hands were to be found in Athens. So I had better show them
the text at once and ask what they could tell me about its date and
writer.

Next would come the history of the text. Unless invented by the
man who wrote the present manuscript, it must have been copied,
more or less accurately, from some earlier manuscript. Could I find
any trace of that? Nothing I had found at Mar Saba seemed relevant, but perhaps there might be something in the big published
catalogue of the Jerusalem library—so many Mar Saba manuscripts had been taken there. That would have to be gone through
carefully and everything on the history of the monastery reviewed
for any hint about a possible author or a situation that might have
favored the production of such a work.

Third was the text itself. The heading said it was by Clement,
but was this true? If not a modern invention, the text still might
have been written by some ancient or medieval author whose name
had been lost, and the attribution to Clement might have been

made by guesswork, by some modern copyist. Medieval Greek manuscripts contain any number of excerpts like this which have had one author's name attached to them by one scribe, another's by another. And of course there were forgers in the middle ages and antiquity, too. This might be an ancient fake, written to be passed off as Clement's by somebody who wanted to invoke the famous father's authority for one or another purpose. All these questions would require a minute analysis of content and style. Every writer has his favorite vocabulary, his favorite ways of saying things, his pet ideas, and it isn't often that these can be imitated accurately. By good luck, a lot of Clement's work had been preserved—three big volumes full. Close comparison of these with the style of the letter ought to yield some pretty strong evidence as to whether or not Clement wrote it.

Finally would come the question of the Gospel. Even if the stylistic evidence indicated that Clement wrote the letter, *he* might have been mistaken about the history of the Gospel text. After all, he was writing about A.D. 180 or 200, well over a century after the time of Mark. And that century had seen a development of all sorts of fantastic forms of Christianity. As the new faith had spread through the Greco-Roman world, men of the most different kinds had seized on its promise of salvation and its story of the saviour and had interpreted the one and retold the other to suit themselves. One result had been a rich crop of Gospels, all of them combining tradition and invention. Four of these Gospels eventually gained general acceptance and were included in the New Testament (the collection of documents approved by the largest of the organized churches). But there had been any number of others that never were so widely accepted. Many were eventually condemned, some just disappeared, half a dozen or so still survive, at least in large part. So the new Gospel text would have to be placed in relation to all this Gospel literature, and especially, of course, in relation to the accepted, "canonical" Gospels. This would show how it stood to the Christian tradition from which all the Gospels derived, and then, at last, I could come to the question, What does it tell us about the tradition and, hence, about Jesus himself?

It was going to be a big job. I sat in the library of the American School in Athens and doodled on my notes as I looked ahead at years of work to come. Circles within circles within circles . . . and what lines of connection could be drawn between them? But no, I certainly was not going to suppress it. It might turn out to be a fake, but even that result would be significant. And fake or not, the puzzle was going to be fun.

4

The Manuscript

The first step was the easiest; I could rely on other scholars' information. Though I knew a little about Greek palaeography, I had no pretense to be an expert on the dating of manuscript hands, particularly modern ones. All I had to do, therefore, was to ask the experts.

I asked Dr. Angelou and Dr. Dimaras at the Greek National Foundation, Dr. Kournoutos at the Greek Department of Education, and Dr. Manousakas at the archives of the Greek Academy. They agreed in dating the text to the eighteenth century. Manousakas and Kournoutos inclined to think it early in the century, possibly even late seventeenth. The others put it later. Angelou was willing to go further and say something about the character of the author: he was probably a monk, since he prefaced his work with the sign of the cross, but he must have been a learned man, since his hand shows the influence of letter forms that were taken up in Greece because of the prestige of western printed editions of Greek texts.

All these scholars emphasized that their opinions were tentative. They referred me to a younger man, Dr. V. Scouvaras, then professor at the Gymnasium in Volos, who was making a special study of the manuscript hands of this period. He was able to date the hand more precisely. It is an example of a type formed at the court of the Oecumenical Patriarch in Constantinople about the middle of the eighteenth century. A date in the second half of that century is therefore most probable.

After getting back to the States I consulted a number of other scholars expert in Greek palaeography[1] and got substantially identical answers. The date of the manuscript may therefore be taken as determined. I doubt that its palaeographic peculiarities will yield much more information.

On the way back to the States I had stopped off to attend a meeting of the international society for New Testament studies. There I took the opportunity to report my discovery to Professor Henry Cadbury, who had been my teacher at Harvard. His reaction was much the same as mine had been: "It is certainly exciting— and may possibly be genuine. Before you say anything about it you had better study it carefully." This I took to heart, as one generally does advice that agrees with one's own decisions.

However, after getting home I asked the opinions of two other great scholars whom it was my good fortune to know well, Erwin Goodenough and A. D. Nock. They were a remarkable pair, the opposite extremes of the English character.

Goodenough was the nonconformist—gaunt, angular, full of individualistic religion (as a youth he had not only been "saved," but "sanctified") and himself protesting against this Protestant background. His revolt had driven him through anthropology to psychoanalysis (Jesus, after his baptism and sanctification, went through the desert to encounter the devil). The result was an astonishing mind, almost monkeylike, constantly curious, always in motion, amazing for its animal intuitions, its ability to leap through the air from fact to fact, and its insouciant resilience if the second fact turned out not to be there. He was Professor of the History of Religion at Yale and had devoted much of his life to a search for mystical elements in ancient Judaism[2]—these were to

1. Professors A. Delatte, M. Richard, G. Soulis, and P. Topping.
2. Though failing to prove his thesis, he revealed a whole side of the religion

be the basis of a work to prove that primitive Christianity was a religion of the free spirit, like his own. Consequently he was predisposed in favor of a discovery that revealed a hidden, potentially mystical side in early Christianity. But he was also a shrewd, realistic denizen of the academic jungle.

"God alone knows what you've got hold of," he said when I finished telling him about the text. "It may not come from Clement, and of course the Gospel won't be Mark. But I'm convinced that it's important. It fits. That's the essential. Wherever it came from, it gives you a glimpse of the esoteric side of the religion, and that's what really matters. And what matters most of all is to know that there *was* an esoteric side."

Nock was the Englishman of the established Church—a huge, fuzzy bear of a man, but a great classical scholar with a mind enormously learned, outstandingly accurate, cautious, balanced, conservative. After an adolescent love affair with Anglo-Catholicism he was safely wedded to "the broad Church," for which he had a deep affection, as he had for everything that made for decency and order. Professor of the History of Religion at Harvard, one of the major campaigns of his scholarly career had been the refutation of attempts to explain the Christian sacraments from the mystery religions. Consequently he was predisposed against a discovery that threatened to reveal an esoteric element at the root of Christianity.

I didn't tell him about the text. I just said, "I have a surprise for you; look at this," and handed him the photographs. (I hope no student ever does that to me!) He passed the test brilliantly. I can still hear him muttering as he bent over the pages, "Ha, Clement! A fragment of a letter, no less. Congratulations! . . . The Carpocratians! I say, this may be important. (My God, this hand is cursive!) 'Carnal and bodily sins' . . . 'slaves of servile desires' . . . Yes, yes, that's what he'd say; that's the language.

---

hitherto almost unknown. See my review article, "Goodenough's 'Jewish Symbols' in Retrospect," *Journal of Biblical Literature* 86(1967)53–66.

. . . This stuff on Mark is excellent. Just what Clement would say; of course he'd defend the Alexandrian position; look at Swete on Mark for that, still the best collection. . . . What's this, 'a more spiritual Gospel'? . . . 'Hierophantic teaching of the Lord'? . . . Well . . . it does sound like Clement . . . I suppose he would use the mystery language; they all borrowed it later. . . . 'Foul demons' . . . 'devising destruction' . . . blasphemous and carnal doctrine,' that rings true again. . . . Yes, now we get the quotations. . . . That's an odd text of Proverbs, you must look that up . . . Good heavens, a Gospel quotation! Oh no, this is too much! No, my dear boy, this can't be genuine. It must be something medieval; fourth or fifth century, perhaps. They made up all sorts of stuff in the fifth century. That's where this will come from; it's not an ancient *flosculum*. But, I say, it is exciting. You must do it up in an article for the *Review*."[3]

"Maybe you're right," I said, "but first of all I'm going to compare the language with that of Clement."

I have related these two interviews because they show two great scholars, with diametrically different attitudes and intellectual qualifications, confronted with important new evidence in the field of their special competence, and reaching immediately the conclusions compatible with their previous positions. Consistency is a frightening virtue. If scholars of the caliber of Goodenough and Nock could react in this way, how far can I trust myself? Not far, I fear, but at least I'm aware of the problem. That is why I look forward to the scholarly discussion that will follow the publication of the text. What will others see in it? And what evidence will they be able to find to support their insights? For the scholars, at least, the matter will come down, in the end, to the question of evidence.

3. *The Harvard Theological Review,* of which he was editor.

5

The Letter

The text broke into three distinct parts: the heading, the letter, and the Gospel quotations. The heading was purely conventional. It might have been written by anybody, even the copyist who wrote the present manuscript. It told me only what its author thought he knew about the following document, *viz:* The letter came from a collection of the letters of Clement, author of the *Stromateis,* and was addressed to Theodore. But were these statements correct?

As to Theodore, there was no telling. Nothing in the text indicated the recipient. No Theodore was conspicuous in Clementine circles. But the name was common and the report might easily be true. The best thing to be said for the name was that nobody had any obvious reason to have put it into the text. A reference to a famous recipient would have been much more suspicious. Who would have forged a letter to a nobody?

As to Clement, the heading could be checked. If Clement wrote the letter it would be in his vocabulary and his style. So all I had to do was compare it, word by word and phrase by phrase, with his recognized works. That was a simple matter . . . it took all my spare time for two years. Computers had not then become generally available for linguistic research; today the actual computation could probably be done in two hours. But it would take me a year to have the texts put on tapes and to proofread the tapes, and I should not learn what I learned about Clement by having to work through his text again and again, looking first for one characteristic, next for another. The mechanization of learning promises to transfer much of it from the minds of scholars to the data banks of machines. The scholar of the future may be one who knows how to consult reference devices, but does not know the primary material.

The work was not entirely unpleasant. Dull as stylistic analysis can be, it is satisfyingly objective. You can work without being troubled by the questions, Am I imagining this? How far is this my prejudice? Am I just making a case? and so on. Either one document uses the same words and phrases as another, or it doesn't. Most of the data are clear, you collect them, you calculate the results, and that's that—"something accomplished, something done." And you have the pleasure of seeing the picture slowly begin to emerge.

What a picture! That was what kept me going through my two years of solitary confinement. In point after point the letter turned out to agree with Clement.

The problem now was to organize the material. First I wrote a commentary on the letter, word by word, collecting the parallels and discussing the dubious points.[1] Nock was a tower of strength in this. His philological knowledge was vast, his judgment impeccable, and his objectivity such that, in spite of his prejudice against Clementine authorship, he often pointed out evidence that went to confirm it. On his advice, when the commentary was finished I sent copies to fourteen scholars either authorities on Clement or generally outstanding in the fields of late classical and patristic Greek, and asked them for corrections and comments.

1. For this commentary and for detailed discussion of the material in this and the following chapters, see my edition of the text, published as *Clement of Alexandria and a Secret Gospel of Mark,* Harvard University Press, 1973. Since the Harvard text has gone through the press very slowly, I have made in the present work a few changes which could not be made there.

(This practice has a good deal to recommend it: if it were generally followed we should have less scholarly publication, and much less misinformation published as scholarship. But the scholars consulted would have no time for work of their own. Recognizing the imposition, I could only plead that I thought the importance of the new text justified it.)

While waiting for the replies to come in, I put together the findings of the commentary in systematic form. To me they seemed, and still seem, practically decisive. The vocabulary of the letter is Clement's; almost all the words are words he uses and many of them are favorites of his, or are used in odd ways in which he also used them. The phrases and the forms of reference and the formulae for beginning sentences are his. The grammatical constructions commonly agree with his usage. The rhythms of the sentence endings are those he favored; those he avoided do not appear. And so on. All this makes it almost impossible that the copyist found an anonymous excerpt and attributed it to Clement merely by a lucky guess. The similarities to Clement's style are so close that they can be explained only in two ways: either this was written by Clement or it is a deliberate and careful imitation, not to say a forgery.

While collecting stylistic data I made a similar study of the details of the content, with similar results. The letter and Clement have much the same notions of Scripture, cite mostly the same books (even with some peculiar readings and interpretations), and use Scripture in the same ways. Both know the classics well and they admire the same authors. Most important, both have the same idea of Christianity. They think of Jesus as a "hierophant," a teacher of mysteries; the believer progresses from the lesser to "the great mysteries" by instruction in secret knowledge (*gnosis*). And both not only claim to have this gnosis, but are hostile to other groups that claim it, the so-called "gnostics." Among these they particularly dislike the Carpocratians, a sect that was prominent only in the second century and that is most prominent in the works of Clement—no other writer gave them so much attention. Finally, there are a number of conspicuous *differences* in points of content between the letter and Clement. Nobody, who knew Clement's style well enough to imitate it in this way, could have been unaware that in these points he was contradicting Clement. Therefore a would-be forger, who wanted to pass the letter off as Clement's, would not have said such things (they are not essential to the content, not points the author seems to be most concerned about). But Clement might have contradicted himself, and as a matter of fact every one of the contradictions can be explained by the supposition that the letter represents Clement's secret teaching, as opposed to that in his published works.

These being the results that emerged from the commentary, I was not much surprised that most of the fourteen scholars consulted thought the letter had probably been written by Clement.[2] Only two, Professors Munck and Völker, thought Clement could not be the author. They did so for technical reasons which I dealt with in revision of the commentary, and shall therefore not discuss here. What troubled me more was that Nock persisted in denying the attribution to Clement, though in the face of the collected evidence he could give no reason for his denial save "instinct." That made me nervous and still does, not only because of Nock's immense knowledge of Greek and his remarkable feeling for Greek style, but also because, apart from his learning, he was a man of unusual intuition.

2. To many of these men my thanks, alas, can no longer be offered, but I wish to record my gratitude to them all: Professors E. Bickerman, W. M. Calder III, H. Chadwick, B. Einarson, L. Früchtel, R. Grant, M. Hadas, W. Jaeger, G. Lampe, C. Mondésert, J. Munck, M. Richard, W. Völker, and A. Wifstrand. Later, the commentary was also read by Professors J. Reumann, C. Richardson, and R. Schippers, all of whom made many helpful observations.

But the other scholars, too, had intuition. And anyhow, in historical questions one has to decide from observable evidence and rational arguments. So I decided to accept, as a working hypothesis, the likelihood that the letter was written by Clement.

With this result of the study, late in 1960, it seemed time to announce the discovery. The annual meeting of the Society of Biblical Literature at the end of that year was an appropriate place for the announcement, and the program committee devoted an evening session to my report on the text and another report on it by Professor Pierson Parker of General Theological Seminary.[3]

3. "A New Gospel Ascribed to Mark," by Sanka Knox, *The New York Times,* December 30, 1960, p. 1; "Expert Disputes 'Secret Gospel,'" by Sanka Knox, *The New York Times,* December 31, 1960, p. 7.

Archimandrite Kyriakos, at whose invitation the author first visited
Mar Saba.

Mar Saba from the opposite side of the canyon. Mar Saba is one of the two great desert monasteries of the Orthodox Church.

Mar Saba from within. With but brief interruptions, there has been some sort of monastic life at this site since the fifth century.

Archimandrite Seraphim.

The view from the tower.

The tower library.

Icons in the cave church.

Manuscript pages pasted together in bindings. The endpaper, here turned down, was a page from a Georgian manuscript. Beneath it is a page from an old Greek manuscript. The leather edge of the binding is seen at the left; the bound, modern Greek manuscript, at the right.

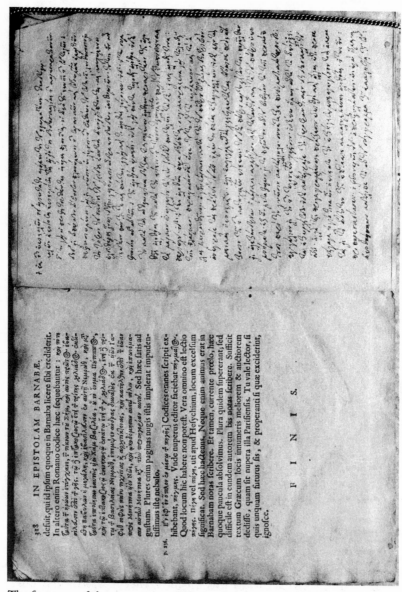

318   IN EPISTOLAM BARNABÆ.

defuit, quid ipsum quoque in Barnaba licere sibi crediderit. In altero enim Romano codice hæc sequebantur : [Greek text] ...

[...] Codices omnes scripti exhibebant, [Greek]. Vnde nuperus editor faciebat [Greek]. Quod locum hic habere non potest. Vera omnino est lectio [Greek], uti apud Hesychium, locum excelsum significat. Sed hæc hactenus. Neque enim animus erat in Barnabam notas scribere. Et tamen, currente prelo, hæc quoque paucula absolvimus. Plura quidem supererant, sed difficile est in eundem autorem his notas scribere. Sufficit textum Græcum locis innumeris meliorem & auctiorem dedisse, quam sit nupera illa Parisiensis. Tu vale lector, si quis unquam futurus sis, & properanti si quæ exciderint, ignosce.

F I N I S.

The first page of the manuscript of Clement's letter, copied into the back of an edition of the letters of St. Ignatius of Antioch.

6

The Gospel: Date and Style

Pierson Parker devoted his report to the Gospel material in the letter. This he did at my request; I had very much wanted his opinion on it. He had written an excellent controversial book on the relation of Matthew to Mark,[1] and he probably knew more about Matthean and Markan style than anybody else in the country. In his discussion of the new material he took as an assumption that Clement had written the letter, and he went on to ask whether or not Clement's statements about the Gospel were correct. His conclusion was that they were not. The style resembled Mark's in some respects, but had so many similarities to other New Testament passages that it seemed likely the author knew a number of the New Testament books. He was probably a Christian who worked in Alexandria somewhat before Clement's time.

Parker's opinion, like Clement's, had to be tested. He had not had the opportunity to study, word by word, all the parallels between the new text and the other early Gospels. Only such study could precisely determine the relationships. So I went back to word counting.

Fortunately, there were some considerations that helped simplify the problem. Not only did Clement's church have this secret Gospel, but the Carpocratians had it, too, though Clement said their

1. *The Gospel before Mark,* Chicago, 1953.

text differed from the text of his own church in a number of points. Clement had to explain both the differences and the common possession of the text. His explanation was that Carpocrates had used magic to enslave a presbyter of "the" (i.e., Clement's) church, had got the text from him, and had then corrupted it to suit his own nefarious ends. This is a cock-and-bull story, most important for what it does not say. It does not say what Clement would gladly have said if he could: that the Carpocratians got the secret Gospel only a few years earlier and had no real claim to it. We know about Carpocrates from a number of ancient references. He must have been at the peak of his activity about A.D. 125 or 130. Clement not only says he used the secret Gospel, but says so in a way that suggests he wrote a commentary on it. We know from another Church father (Irenaeus of Lyons) that the Carpocratians did have a commentary on secret sayings attributed to Jesus. Therefore Carpocrates probably did use the secret Gospel. Therefore the secret Gospel was probably in existence before his time. On these grounds it would have been written before 120 at the latest; a more likely date for its composition would be somewhere around 100.

This meant that I could leave out of consideration the Gospels of the mid-second century and later. The new text belonged to the period in which the canonical Gospels themselves were taking or had just taken form—they date approximately between 75 and 100—so its relation to them was the thing to be investigated.

Once I started to think along these lines, a new way of stating the problem occurred to me: What was the relation of the secret Gospel to canonical Mark? Clement says it was an expansion. He declares (what many believed in antiquity) that Mark wrote the canonical Gospel in Rome during the last years of Peter's life there. Then, after Peter's death, Clement says, Mark came to Alexandria, bringing with him both his own and Peter's notes. From these "he transferred to his former book" additional material, not, indeed, the most secret teachings of Jesus, but stories and sayings of which the interpretation would lead initiates toward the secret. This means that the secret Gospel, as Clement knew it, contained all of canonical Mark *plus* additional material, both stories and sayings. The Carpocratian text, according to Clement, contained yet more additions, some of which he calls "falsifications." The term proves he disliked them; it is not reliable evidence about their origin.

Do we know any other expanded forms of the text of Mark? Yes, indeed we do. The canonical Gospels of Matthew and Luke are generally thought by scholars to be such expansions. Both of them contain most of the text of Mark with some abbreviations and omissions, but with large insertions.

Thus the secret Gospel might be seen as a new element in the history of the text of Mark. We might suppose that Mark took approximately its present form shortly after 70. Then it began to be expanded in different areas. By about 100, we may say, three expanded texts had been roughly stabilized—one in Syria, another in Asia Minor, another in Egypt. The expansions produced in Syria and Asia Minor have been preserved; they are our canonical Gospels of Matthew and Luke, repectively. But in Egypt Christianity ran wild in a tangle of secret religious societies, the "gnostic" sects. Each of these developed its own Gospel (or Gospels) and usually tried to keep it (or them) secret. Consequently, though a number of the Egyptian texts probably stemmed from a single expansion (as Clement's secret Gospel and that of the Carpocratians certainly did), none of them ever gained such general acceptance as did Matthew and Luke. When gnosticism was killed out, they died with it.

This was beautifully simple and plausible, but that didn't prove it true. The history of the Gospel texts was not a one-way street. There had been abbreviations, as well as expansions. So if Clement was wrong about the origin of his text, he might also be wrong about its relation to canonical Mark. What if the secret text had been earlier, and canonical Mark had been cut down from it? There was one place, in particular, where it looked as if this had happened. In Mk. 10.46 the canonical text reads, "And *they* come into Jericho. And when *he* was leaving Jericho" . . . So what happened in Jericho? One might say, Nothing. But just there Clement's secret Gospel located a short story, and the Carpocratian text had a longer one.

So there was nothing to do but to keep on comparing the text word by word and phrase by phrase with the canonical Gospels, and to try to see in each instance what the relation actually was. The problem was terribly complicated because the Gospels are written so largely in formulae that recur again and again. The early churches, like contemporary Communist groups, spoke a jargon of their own. The Gospels are the deposit of this peculiar language. Clichés turn up everywhere, so literary dependence cannot be proved by parallels which would ordinarily seem sufficient evidence of it. The chances are that there will be half a dozen more parallels to the same phrase. Only when *all* the parallels and *all* the phrases have been considered can one put the results together and see what the relations of the texts really were.

Another year and a half went by, and once again patterns began to emerge, no less definite than before, but this time more puzzling. First of all it became clear that the new text was very close to Mark, far closer than to any other Gospel. Parker had not seen this because his sampling of the material had been too small and, for the samples he had chosen, he had considered only the closest parallels. When *all* the relevant passages were taken into account, a quite different picture appeared. The vocabulary, phraseology, and grammatical peculiarities of the new text were all of them predominantly Markan. There was almost nothing in it that Mark could not have written.[2] There were almost no traits that indicated

2. The one important exception is the final clause, "and Jesus did not receive them," of which the Greek contains a characteristically Lukan verb used in a

knowledge of any Gospel save Mark, and the few exceptions could easily be explained by textual corruption. Finally, the new text was connected with Mark by half a dozen major verbal parallels. All this pointed to Markan authorship. But there was one very serious objection. The text was more like Mark than a section of Mark should be. It had too many Markan words, too many parallels to other passages of the Gospel. This looked like the result of imitation.

But if the secret Gospel was an imitation of Mark, it must have been a very early one. Besides the report that Carpocrates had used it, evidence turned up to show that knowledge of it had influenced the copyists of New Testament texts in Egypt before 150. Yet more, there were a few passages in Matthew and Luke that seemed to show knowledge of this material. Those in Matthew were sufficiently numerous and peculiar to make the supposition of knowledge seem likely. Another piece of evidence that pointed to an early date was the fact that the secret Gospel had very few Matthean or Lukan elements. Matthew and Luke seem to have eclipsed Mark very early; it is hard to believe that even in Egypt a Gospel written after 125 would not have shown more Matthean and Lukan traits.

On stylistic and historical grounds, therefore, the secret Gospel quoted by Clement would seem to have been almost what Clement said it was: an expansion of Mark made, if not by Mark himself, at least by a disciple of his who imitated his style very closely. The writer lived in Egypt, almost certainly before 125, and probably well before it (so early, in fact, that his additions were known to Matthew and Luke, who are commonly thought to have written somewhere around 90).

These conclusions were not wholly conclusive. Clement's quota-

---

sense hardly to be found in Christian literature before the second century. But there are strong reasons for thinking this clause an addition, perhaps by Clement himself, to cover a gap left by the deletion of unpleasant material. This passage will be discussed later on.

tions of the secret Gospel were very short. There was no telling how far the passages quoted were typical of the rest. I could see that the external evidence and the evidence from style would have to be checked by consideration of the content. And here came the most exciting discovery.

7

The Gospel: Relation to John

As soon as I read the manuscript I saw that the resurrection story in it was a variant of the story of Lazarus. The essentials were all there: the sister whose brother had died comes to ask Jesus' help, they go to the tomb, the stone is removed, the dead man is raised and comes out of the tomb.

This, by itself, was interesting, because in the canonical Gospels the Lazarus story is found only in John, and John is the odd one of the four. Matthew and Luke keep at least the main outline of the Markan story; the material they add is roughly similar in style to that in Mark and gives a generally similar picture of Jesus. You can put the three side by side in parallel columns and see at a glance what each has added or left out; this is why they are called the "syn-optic" Gospels—the Gospels that can all be seen at once. John is quite different. The outline of the earlier chapters is completely alien to Mark's; most of the Markan stories never appear; there are a number of important stories of which the synoptics know nothing; the style is conspicuously different and so is the picture of Jesus.

Consequently the relation of John to the synoptics has long been disputed. (Can both be true? If not, which is to be preferred?) In this argument the Lazarus story plays an important part. It relates one of the most miraculous miracles in all the Gospels, the great example of the resurrection (which for Paul was the foundation of the Christian faith, I Cor. 15.17). If Jesus did raise Lazarus, the opponents of John said, how is it possible that the synoptics should never have mentioned this marvel; but if he did not, what must we think of John?

Therefore, to find the story in Clement's secret Gospel was a real surprise, because the secret Gospel was unquestionably of synoptic type and style. Here was evidence that the Lazarus story was known to the synoptic tradition, and here, too, was an explanation of its absence from the canonical synoptics: it was part of the secret teaching and they were written for outsiders.

This much I talked over with Professor Parker while he was preparing his paper. He undertook to investigate the problem further. His strength is to pay close attention to details, but in this case they misled him. He found that more details of the new story were paralleled in the cure of the demoniac in Mk. 5.1–20 than in the Lazarus story of John; therefore he supposed the new story patterned on Mk. 5.1–20. But this neglects the content of the stories and the content is the essential thing. Mere similarities of detail occur constantly between most of the resurrection and healing stories because of their common subject matter. There are, for instance, more parallels of detail between the Lazarus story in John and the raising of Jairus' daughter in Mk. 5.22–43 than there are between the new resurrection story and the cure of the demoniac in Mk. 5.1–20. But nobody would suppose John's Lazarus story modeled on Mark's story of Jairus' daughter.

The essential structure of the resurrection story in the secret Gospel had to be compared with that of the Lazarus story in John. The way to do this was to put the two in parallel columns. As soon as I started to do so I saw that the contexts of both were part of the problem. In the latter half of John the outline of the Gospel runs roughly parallel to that of Mark. Each one has big sections that the other lacks, but the connecting passages and consequently the outlines of Jesus' travels are surprisingly similar. Parker had observed that the Lazarus story in John and the resurrection story in the secret Gospel occur at the same period in Jesus' career: Jesus has gone up from Galilee to Judea and thence to Transjordan. I now saw that the framework of Mk. 10.1–34 *plus* the resurrection story of the secret Gospel was parallel to the framework of Jn. 10.40–11.54 *plus* the Lazarus story. This means that the secret Gospels *fits* the Markan framework at that place at which Clement said it stood in Mark!

But that was only the beginning. When I got the two texts side by side, what I saw was this:

Mk.	*Jn.*
10.1: And arising thence, he comes into the territories of Judea and beyond the Jordan, and crowds again come together to him, and as his custom was, he again taught them.	10.40: And he went away again beyond the Jordan, into the place where John was at first baptizing. And he remained there. (41) And many came to him. And they said, "John did no sign, but all things which John said about this man were true." (42) And many believed in him there.
2–12 Dispute on divorce. 13–16 Blessing children. 17–23 The rich young ruler. 24–31 Sayings on rewards.	
	11.1: And there was a sick [man], Lazarus, from Bethany, from the village of Mary and Martha her sister. (2) It was Mary who anointed the Lord with myrrh and dried his feet with her hair, whose brother Lazarus was sick. (3) Conse-

Mk.

Jn.

quently the sisters sent to him, saying, "Lord, behold, he whom you love is sick." (4) But Jesus, hearing [this], said, "This sickness is not unto death, but for the glory of God, that the Son of God may be glorified by it." (5) Now Jesus loved Martha and her sister and Lazarus. (6) However, when he heard that he is sick, he then remained two days in the place where he was. (7) Then, after this, he says to the disciples, "Let us go into Judea again." (8) The disciples say to him, "Rabbi, just now the Jews tried to stone you, and you are going there again?" (9) Jesus answered, "Are there not twelve hours in the day? If one walk about during the day he does not stumble, because he sees the light of this world. (10) But if one walk about during the night he stumbles, because the light is not in him."

32: And they were in the road going up to Jerusalem, and Jesus was going before them, and they marvelled, and those who were following were afraid. And taking aside the twelve, he began to tell them the things which were about to happen to him, (33) "Behold, we are going up to Jerusalem, and the Son of Man will be handed over to the high priests and the scribes, and they will condemn him to death and will hand him over to the gentiles. (34) And they will mock him and spit on him and scourge him,

and they will kill [him]

(11) These things he said, and after this he says to them, "Lazarus, our friend, has fallen

Mk.

and after three days he will
arise."

The Secret Text

And they come

into Bethany, and

a certain woman,

whose brother

had died, was there.

Jn.

asleep, but I am going in order
that I may wake him." (12) So
the disciples said to him, "Lord,
if he has fallen asleep, he will be
well." (13) But Jesus had
spoken about his death. They,
however, thought, he is speaking
about falling asleep in slumber.
(14) Therefore Jesus then said
to them openly, "Lazarus has
died, (15) and I am glad—on
your account, that you may believe—that I was not there. But
let us go to him." (16) Then
Thomas, who was called "the
twin," said to his fellow disciples, "Let us go, too, that we
may die with him." (17) Jesus,
then, coming, found him already
four days in the tomb. (18) And
Bethany was near Jerusalem—
less than two miles away. (19)
Consequently, many of the Jews
had come to Martha and Mary,
to console them about their
brother. (20) Now Martha,
when she heard that Jesus is
coming, went to meet him. But
Mary sat in the house. (21)
Martha then said to Jesus,
"Lord, if you were here my
brother would not have died.
(22) And now I know that
whatever you ask God, God will

The Secret Text

Jn.

give you." (23) Jesus says to
her, "Your brother will arise."
(24) Martha says to him, "I
know that he will arise in the
resurrection in the last day."
(25) Jesus said to her, "I am
the resurrection and the life,
Whoever believes in me, even if
he die, shall live, (26) and
everyone who lives and believes
in me shall not die forever. Do
you believe this?" (27) She says
to him, "Yes, Lord, I have believed that you are the Messiah,
the Son of God, the Coming
One, [who is coming] into the
world." (28) And saying this
she went off and called Mary,
her sister, secretly, saying, "The
Teacher is here and calls you."
(29) She, when she heard, gets
up quickly and came to him.
(30) Jesus had not yet come
into the village, but was still in
the place where Martha met
him. (31) Now the Jews who
were with her in the house and
were consoling her, seeing that
Mary quickly got up and went
out, followed her, thinking,
"She goes to the tomb, to weep
there." (32) However Mary,

And, coming, she
prostrated herself

when she came where Jesus was,
seeing him, fell at his feet, say-

The Secret Text

before Jesus and says to
him "Son of David, have
mercy on me." But the
disciples rebuked her.
And Jesus
being angered,
went off with her into
the garden

where the tomb was. And
straightway a great cry
was heard from the tomb. And
going near, Jesus rolled away
the stone from the door of the
tomb. And straightway,

Jn.

ing to him, "Lord, if you were
here, my brother would not have
died." (33) Jesus therefore,
when he saw her weeping, and
the Jews, who came with her,
weeping, fumed in spirit and
was troubled (34) and said,
"Where have you put him?"
They say to him. "Lord, come
and see." (35) Jesus wept. (36)
The Jews therefore said, "See
how he loved him!" (37) And
some of them said, "Was not
this [fellow], who opened the
eyes of the blind [man], able to
do [something] so that this
[man], too, should not die?
(38) Jesus, therefore, again
fuming within himself, comes
to the tomb. It was a cave, and
a stone lay upon it. (39) Jesus
says, "Take away the stone." The
sister of the dead man, Martha,
says to him, "Lord, he already
stinks, for he is in his fourth
day." (40) Jesus says to her,
"Did I not say to you that if
you believe you shall see the
glory of God?" (41) So they
took away the stone. And Jesus
lifted up his eyes and said,
"Father, I thank you that you
heard me. (42) And I knew
that you always hear me. But I

The Secret Text

going in where the youth was, he
stretched forth his hand and
raised him, seizing his hand.
But the youth, looking upon
him, loved him, and began to
beseech him that he might
be with him. And
going out of the tomb,
they came into the house of the
youth, for he was rich.

The nocturnal initiation.

And thence, arising,
he returned to the other side
of the Jordan.

Jn.

spoke because of the crowd
standing around, that they may
believe that you sent me." (43)
And saying these words, he
uttered a great cry, "Lazarus,
come out!" (44) The dead man
came out, bound hand and foot
with bandages, and his face was
wrapped with a towel. Jesus says
to them, "Loose him and let
him go."

45–53 The Jews' reaction and
plot.
54: Jesus therefore no longer
went about openly among the
Jews, but went thence into the
district near the desert, into
a town called Ephraim, and remained there with the disciples.

What does all this show? It shows that the story in the secret
Gospel is older than the story in John. How does it show that?
Let us look at the texts:

Mk. 10.1 and Jn. 10.40 are clearly parallel. John has built up
his version by adding a slap at the Baptist (in verse 41). Some of
the Baptist's followers claimed that he was the Messiah, so John
lost no opportunity to insist that he was merely an inferior forerunner of Jesus; this addition is one of a well-known series, all of
them certainly the work of John.

In Mk. 10.2–31 we have a series of Mark's additions, unparalleled in John. Only the last two of these are connected by a
narrative thread (and that thread was added by Mark), but they

lead up thematically to Jesus' prophecy of his passion and resurrection (32–34), and the promise of the resurrection is confirmed by the immediately following resurrection story in the secret text of Mark. The whole section (10.1–34 + secret text) thus has, roughly, a unified structure. But it is made up of units of typically synoptic form—short stories with characters that come out of nowhere and vanish into nothing, sayings with the briefest possible settings, or none at all. This is the way the synoptic authors usually work: their larger structures are commonly mere *collages* of the short stories and sayings furnished them by the tradition, with only minor additions here and there.

John, by contrast, has built up the resurrection story into a coherent romance. Instead of one sister, he has two—doubling characters is a well-known secondary trait in Gospel stories; here it makes possible a varied narrative with contrast and conversation, psychological and moral and theological interests all unknown to the simple, primitive miracle story. The sisters and the brother are named and located in a named town and identified with figures who have appeared in other stories—locating stories, naming unknown characters, and identifying unrelated ones are also recognized secondary traits. The story has personal emotional interest—Jesus loved Lazarus; it pauses for Jesus to give theological explanations (11.4, etc.); it has suspense—he did not go at once, and when he did go it was at the risk of his life. As usual in John, Jesus speaks in metaphors, the disciples do not understand him, he therefore has and takes the opportunity to explain himself. Finally there is a touching expression of the disciples' loyalty to Jesus (11.16), as an example to John's fellow Christians; persecutions are in the offing. All this romantic-theological-moral introduction is John's work. We can only guess that in the text he had before him, as in Mark, a prophecy of the passion preceded the story of the resurrection; John therefore included the theme in his retelling (11.7–10).

In the same way John has reworked the story of the secret text, which now follows. He specifies that Lazarus had been dead four days in the tomb; this proves he was really dead and proves the raising was a miracle. (We know that the resurrection stories were attacked in antiquity by critics who claimed that the bodies were not really dead.) John adds statistics (the distance of Bethany from Jerusalem) and explanations (that was why the Jews could come) —he loves such pseudo-historicity, but sometimes gets his facts wrong, as here. He brings on the Jews as a tragic chorus; they provide additional dramatic interest, witnesses to the miracles, and a foil to Jesus—their usual functions in John. Here again the action is interrupted by a conversation (11.22–27) which is pure Johannine theology. Then the other sister is introduced for contrast and the action takes up from the very place at which it left off (11.21 = 11.32). After the touching account of Jesus' emotion (33–35) the Jews are made to sneer at his love for Lazarus and use Lazarus' death to discredit his powers (36–37). Then John again goes back to his source ("fumed in spirit"/"fuming within himself": 11.33 = 11.38). Finally we get to the miracle, but not before Martha has again insisted that Lazarus really has been four days dead, and Jesus has prefaced his action with an unnecessary stage-whisper to his Father, explaining the details. All of this is obvious, unmistakable Johannine elaboration. If any further proof of the fact were needed, the Greek style of these verses would supply it— they are full of typically Johannine words and phrases.

When all this characteristically Johannine material is taken away, what is left is a story much like the one in the secret Gospel: A sister (whose brother had died) went to meet Jesus and fell at his feet and said to him, "Lord, if you were here, my brother would not have died." Jesus, when he saw her weeping, fumed in himself and came to the tomb. It was a cave and a stone lay upon it. Jesus said, "Take away the stone." So they took away the stone. And Jesus uttered a great cry, "Come out!" The dead man came out.[1] This is the essential story that was used by John; it has none of John's typical theological vocabulary.

From here on, the texts diverge. The initiation story of the secret Gospel is not in John; the story of the Jews' plot is not in the secret Gospel. But both sections conclude with the same piece of framework: after this, Jesus went back to the edge of the desert. (John again names the town; the secret Gospel merely says, "beyond the Jordan.")

All this leads to the conclusion that Jn. 10.40–11.54 is a reworking of a collection of stories much like those in Mk. 10.1 + 32–34 + the secret Gospel.

The next questions are, How did the stories that John reworked differ from those in Mark and the secret Gospel, and which were earlier?

Here the answers are not quite so clear, because it is hard to be sure how many of the differences between the stories are due to changes made by John. For instance, John was probably afraid the cry from the tomb (originally the scream of Death, a demon about to be robbed of its prey?) might be used as evidence that Lazarus was not really dead; he therefore transferred the cry to Jesus. Other suspicious traits, like the odd expression "fumed in himself," raise more complicated problems which cannot here be discussed.

Some differences, however, probably go back to John's source. For instance, in the secret Gospel the sister appeals to Jesus with the words, "Son of David, have mercy on me." In John the sister says, "Lord, if you were here, my brother would not have died." John certainly found this phrase in his source, because he came back to it after a theological insertion (11.21 = 11.32). Now, "Son of David, have mercy" expressed the primitive Palestinian

---

1. Notice that here, when copying his source, John says only "the dead man," not "Lazarus." The grave clothes may be another Johannine addition to prove the man was dead. That he was bound in them contradicts the statement that he came out of the tomb. Is this careless invention or early contamination with another version?

hope for immediate action by a present Davidic Messiah. The cry
and the title therefore disappeared when the Gospel moved out
of its early Palestinian milieu. But, "Lord, if you were here, my
brother would not have died" is a cry of grief from the Church
after Jesus' death, and an expression of hope in a future resurrection. The text in the secret Gospel seems to be, at least in this detail, older than the source used by John.

About other differences it is harder to decide. Most of them
could be explained by John's well-known motives, but some of
them, nevertheless, may be due to his source. John's motives were
not wholly peculiar; he shared the concerns and prejudices of many
Christians of his time, so the story as it came to him may have already been altered by others in ways he would have found congenial. Thus the secret Gospel makes Jesus move the stone himself; John makes others move it—manual labor was thought de-
grading. The secret Gospel makes Jesus go into the tomb and raise
the dead by hand; in John he merely gives the order and the dead
man rises; the miracle has grown with age. Whatever their origins,
these differences strengthen the impression that the resurrection
story in the secret Gospel appears in a form not only older than the
present text of John, but even older than the story John used as
his source.

As if this conclusion weren't enough, another followed. (There
were just a few wonderful days in which everything began to fit
together.) The continued parallelism, between Jn. 10.40–11.54 and
Mk. 10.1–34 + the secret Gospel, proved Clement was right in his
placing of the secret Gospel section in Mark. But with this section
so placed, I now could see that the whole latter halves of Mark
and John ran parallel. Here they are:

Mk.	Jn.
6.32: And they went off in the boat . . .	6.1: After these things Jesus went off beyond the sea . . .

Mk.		*Jn.*
The feeding of the 5,000.	=	The feeding of the 5,000.
6.45 And straightway he compelled his disciples to enter the boat and go ahead to the other side, to Bethsaida 6.46 And . . . he went off into the hills to pray.		6.16f. And when it was late his disciples came down to the sea and entering a boat they came beyond the sea into Capernaum (6.15 Jesus then . . . went away again into the hills by himself.)
The walking on the sea.	=	The walking on the sea.
6.54f. And . . . [the people], as soon as they recognized him, ran together . . .		6.24f. The crowd . . . came into Capernaum looking for Jesus and when they found him . . .
Summary: Jesus' miracles of healing.	? =	Discussion: Jesus is the bread of life.
The dispute on handwashing.		
Trip to the territory of Tyre.		
The Syrophoenician.		
Return to Galilee.		
The dumb man.		
The feeding of 4,000.		
The demand for a sign.		
The leaven of the Pharisees.		
The blind man of Bethsaida.		
8.27–30 Peter's confession.	=	6.66–69 Peter's confession.
Peter is Satan.	=	Judas is a devil.
The sayings on self-sacrifice.		
The transfiguration.		
The demoniac boy.		
9.30f. And going out from there they traveled about through Galilee . . . For he taught his disciples . . . that the Son of Man is given over into the hands of men and they will kill him . . .		7.1 And after these things Jesus went about in Galilee. For he did not want to go about in Judea because the Jews wanted to kill him.

Mk.

Jn.
Jesus' brothers taunt him.

The dispute on precedence.
The stranger who exorcized.
The saying on scandals.
10.1a And thence arising
he comes into the hill country
of Judea,

7.10 But when his brothers went
up [to Jerusalem] to the feast,
then he too went up . . .
The disputes in Jerusalem.
The man born blind.
The sayings on the door to the
sheepfold.
The appeal to the witness of his
works.

10.1b and beyond the Jordan,
and crowds again came together
to him.
The question on divorce.
The blessing on children.
The rich young ruler.
The saying on scandals.

10.40f. And he went away again
beyond Jordan . . . and many
came to him.

10.32 And they were in the
road going up to Jerusalem,
and Jesus was going before
them, and they were amazed
and those who followed were
afraid.
Jesus' prophecy of his own
death and resurrection.

Secret text: The Lazarus story.
The nocturnal initiation.

Secret text: And thence . . . he

The preface to the Lazarus story.
11.7f. Then . . . he says to the
disciples, "Let us go into Judea
again." The disciples say to him,
"Rabbi, just now the Jews tried
to stone you, and you are going
there again?"
=   Jesus' announcement of Lazarus'
death and prophecy of his resurrection.
=   The Lazarus story.

The Jews' reaction and plot.
11.54 So Jesus no longer went

Mk.	*Jn.*
returned to the other side of the Jordan.	about openly among the Jews, but went thence into the district near the desert, into a town called Ephraim . . .
(The Jews' reactions, Mk. 14.1 f.)	= More of the Jews' reactions.
Mk. The question of James and John.	
Secret text: The events in Jericho.	
Mk. Bartimaeus.	
(The anointing in Bethany, Mk. 14.3–11.)	= The anointing in Bethany.
The entry of Jerusalem.	= The entry of Jerusalem.
The cursing of the fig tree.	
The cleansing of the temple.	= (The cleansing of the temple, Jn. 2.14–17.)
The fig tree found withered.	
The question as to Jesus' authority.	= (The question as to Jesus' authority, Jn. 2.18.)
The parable of the rented vineyard.	
Questions by Herodians, Sadducees, and a scribe.	
The question as to the Son of David.	
The warning against scribes.	
The widow's mite.	
The prophecy of the destruction of the temple.	= (The prophecy of the destruction of the temple, Jn. 2.19–22.)
The prophecy of the end.	
The Jews' reactions.	= (More of the Jews' reactions, Jn. 11.55–7f.)
The anointing in Bethany.	= (The anointing in Bethany, Jn. 12.1–8.)

Mk.	*Jn.*
	The request of the Greeks.
	The Evangelist on the Jews.
	Jesus' declaration of his mission.
The preparation for the last supper.	
	The footwashing.
The last supper.	= The last supper.
The passion story.	= The passion story.

The remarkable things in this list are the continued parallelism of the geographical items of the framework and the near identity in order of those major elements the two Gospels have in common (those marked by the equals sign). One group of these appears in John in chapter 2, but even there they appear in the same order as in Mk. 11–13. Besides the similarities of episodes and framework, there is an even more important similarity in their relationship: in both Gospels the parallel episodes stand in the same relation to the parallel framework—the same episodes occur not only in the same order, but also in the same places in the geographical frame. Yet both the parallel episodes and the parallel geographical notices differ so widely from each other in wording and in many details that it is almost impossible to think either Gospel based on the other. Their differences confirm the supposition of independence to which the evidence of the secret text already led us. We might suppose they derived from a common oral tradition—but could an oral tradition account for so long an agreement in order, and for the similarity in content (without much similarity in wording) of the many little geographical notices?

It seems more likely to suppose that behind both Gospels lay some common document, perhaps in Aramaic. Differences of translation would then account for the differences of wording, but agreement in content. Using different translations, probably altered yet further by copyists' mistakes, both Mark and John would have inserted into them at different places the material peculiar to their own Gospels. Also, each may have omitted or reworked parts of the common text.

We cannot be sure that only the stories found in both Mark and John belonged to their common source; some of the stories peculiar to one or the other *may* have come from it. But we can be almost sure that the stories they both have *did* come from it. Now the resurrection story of the secret text occurs in the same place in the outlines of both, and both introduce it by similar pieces of framework, and both have similar notices following it. So the resurrection story was almost certainly part of the common source which both Mark and John used. Whether or not the initiation story was in the common source, there is no telling. If it was, John must have omitted it, as he did the story of the essential actions in the last supper.

If the resurrection story was in Mark's source it was probably in the earliest form of Mark. If so, the canonical text of Mark would have been produced by abbreviation; the secret text would have been earlier.

Curiously, I have no memory of the days when all this became clear. The experience I shall never forget—it was probably the high point of my life. But the other things that must have been happening at the same time are simply gone, hidden by the blaze of the facts, like stars in the day. I know it happened in the spring of 1963. I think I remember the strange feeling of walking around the unchanged world, doing the usual things, unnoticed and unnoticeable, with all of this going on inside my head.

Soon, however, the blaze of invisible light revealed that my findings contradicted each other. The stylistic study had led me to conclude that the secret Gospel was a secondary expansion of Mark, a very early continuation, based on the same tradition and closely— too closely—imitating Mark's style. Now the study of the relation to John indicated that the resurrection story of the secret Gospel, at very least, had been in the source both Mark and John had used It therefore must have been earlier than Mark.

This contradiction was made even sharper by what I had learned in the meanwhile about the relation between the content of the secret Gospel and that of the neighboring passages of Mark. Here, though, the decisive discovery had not been mine, but Professor Cyril Richardson's.

8

The Gospel: Content

The announcement of the manuscript's discovery in 1960 had brought considerable correspondence. Some of this was merely amusing. Here are samples from three letters; there were many more.

It is sickening to read, in this age of great advance in science and medicine, of an educator dishing out such garbage.

Your finding of Clement's transcribed testimony to a "secret Gospel" of Mark was by no chance, for it fits into the picture of a divine plan to unfold that "secret" with all its implications for our world.

It can be dangerous. One would indeed have to use caution in explaining to others. It is magnetic—hence electrical—a grounded short circuit can happen so fast.

Other letters, however, led to valuable help. Professor Schippers of Amsterdam, in particular, wrote to inquire about the Gospel text, and he and his pupil, Professor Baarda, subsequently contributed a number of important observations on its relation to the textual history of the New Testament. This new subject matter was significant: my research was moving away from the fields of classical philology and patristics to that of New Testament criticism. Nock's death early in 1963—a loss of which I am still sensible—made this move sharper, for he had been my principal adviser in the classical field. Also, when I completed the stylistic commentary on the Gospel text, in late summer of 1962, I sent copies to a number of New Testament scholars,[1] and in the winter of 1962–63 it was studied by the Columbia New Testament Seminar, whose members contributed many corrections.

By far the most important development, however, was due to Richardson. He was Professor of Church History at Union Theological Seminary, across the street from Columbia. I knew and respected his work, and had known him slightly for some time, but we had never been close. Perhaps the worst side of the study of history is that it leaves one so little time for the living. In a great university you are surrounded by fascinating people who have no time to talk to you, and to whom you, if interested in your own field, have no time to talk. Consequently, when Richardson came up to me after the SBL meeting and asked if he might see a copy of the new material, I was a bit surprised, but of course I sent him the text.

Two weeks later I received a four-page letter of which the most important section read as follows:

A Possible Thesis regarding the Gospel Perikope[2]

I should like to suggest that the perikope of Mk. 10.13–45 is that for the Paschal vigil in Clement's church. [In antiquity this "vigil"—an all-night service preceding Easter day—was the occasion when baptisms were performed.] The purpose of the insertion would be to show that the rich man *can* be saved, and thus to off-set the previous story. If Clement's group were reasonably well-off, this part of the chapter would surely have been a stumbling block, especially if it were used at Christian baptism.

In favor of this thesis are the following facts:

1. I owe thanks for particular help to Professors P. Benoit, H. J. Cadbury, W. M. Calder III (a solitary classicist), G. Kilpatrick, H. Koester, C. Moule, P. Parker, J. Reumann, and K. Stendahl.
2. *Perikope* is a technical term of New Testament criticism; it means "section."

(a) The insertion was read only *in the course of* the "great mysteries." I take this to mean baptism, to which Clement applies all degrees of mystery language . . .

(b) The whole section is suggestive of baptism:

(1) *Blessing of the children.* This story is surely told to defend infant baptism . . .

(2) *The rich man.* Emphasis on the commandments.[3]

(3) *Passion and resurrection* prediction.

(4) *The insertion of a resurrection and a baptism.*[4] . . . The contrast with the other rich man whom Jesus loved is clear in that this one *loves Jesus* and wants to be with him.

(5) *The cup and the baptism* of the James and John story—highly appropriate to the Paschal vigil and first Eucharist.

(c) Why is Clement so exercised about the salvation of the rich in [his tract] *What Rich Man Can be Saved?* And why does he depart from his usual practice and cite the whole story from *Mark* in that tract? These questions can be answered if the story of the rich man was always raising difficulties for the newly baptised. The secret perikope (as well as Clement's tract) were aimed to overcome them.

(d) The scheme in the letter is:

(1) *Ordinary Mark* for catechumens,[5] to whom faith is appropriate.

(2) *Mark with secret insertions* for baptism at the Paschal vigil.

(3) *The unwritten tradition* for the true gnostic. Mark did not write down or divulge this.

That was it, in a nutshell. I was suspicious at first—as one usually is of other people's discoveries—but a long conversation (the first of many) sufficed to convince me and a month later I was writing Nock:

Richardson at Union has made a brilliant analysis of the content and role of the longer quotation. He supposes that Clement's church in Alexandria was formed by the coming together of Christian congrega-

3. The ten commandments were traditionally an important part of baptismal teaching.
4. I.e., the resurrection and initiation stories of the secret Gospel.
5. Persons receiving instruction preparatory to baptism.

tions of different sorts, most of them poor literalists, but some of them well-to-do, with strong philosophic or gnostic elements. These latter groups accepted the beliefs and rites of the simple as permissible and sufficient for a sort of salvation, but held to their own theories privately as the explanation of the higher truth and kept their own rites—baptism and eucharist—as higher mysteries into which properly prepared Christians might be initiated.

This analysis enables him to read Mk. 10.13–45 as a baptismal perikope, as follows: Suffer the little children to come unto me. What—*more* than keep the commandments—must I do to be saved? Give up all and follow me. But the rich are unwilling to make the sacrifice and are lost. What shall the followers have? Rewards, and life everlasting. This promise is confirmed by the resurrection story in the secret Gospel, so the following initiation was a baptism, and the story of James and John, after that, sets the theme of the baptismal sermon: the rewards will be given not only to the first apostles, but to all those who are baptized and drink of the cup of the eucharist; but be humble, for the Son of Man came in humility as a saviour.

The one element in this which would most bother Clement's circle of prosperous gnostics would be the loss of the rich young man. We know it did bother them, because Clement wrote *What Rich Man Can be Saved?* to answer the difficulty. In that he quotes the story at length from Mark, though his favorite Gospels were Matthew, John, and Luke. Why quote from Mark? Because in his secret [Gospel of] Mark this section had been made to show that even the rich man who at first rejected Jesus, although dead and buried in the world, could still be saved by the miracle of the resurrection and could receive the true, gnostic baptism, for which one came in the proper baptismal garb, a white sheet over the naked body.

All this seems to me to fit together too well to be accident, and it has an interesting confirmation: I haven't yet had time to study in detail the New Testament parallels to the stories quoted, but I sent the text to Father Benoit[6] and he made a preliminary study immediately. From

6. Father P. Benoit, O.P., of the École biblique et archéologique française de Jérusalem.

his study it seems that the only Lukan trace of any importance in the longer story is the phrase "for he was rich," which I think, therefore, probably a gloss, added in the reworking of the story for the purpose Richardson suggests.

All this has me considerably excited. Perhaps it's just as well I have two jobs that must be done at once before I can get back to study of the letter, which I hope to do by the end of next month. In the meanwhile I am of course keeping my eyes open for materiai relevant to apocryphal Gospels, and I should be particularly grateful for any advice you could give me about the following questions:

What evidence is there for destruction of apocryphal gospels . . . by ecclesiastical or, after the triumph of the Church, secular authorities? (I don't suppose I need "after the triumph of the Church" in that sentence. No doubt the Roman authorities destroyed gnostic Gospels, during the persecutions, with as much enthusiasm as they did orthodox.)

Do you know anything showing application to prose material—e.g., folktales—of the sort of analysis of compositions by formulae which Parry and Lord have used on the Homeric poems? Notopoulos,[7] who is a member of that school, talked here about the Homeric Hymns and his demonstration of how they broke down into strings of formulae looked exactly like the sort of thing I expect to get on analysis of the quotations in the letter. I asked him about folk tales and he said they were certainly composed in the same way, but he didn't know of any studies. Of course . . . [some of those] working on the Gospel text take it for granted that anything similar to the canonical Gospels is derivative, and anything not similar, secondary. Thus they cover the field completely with only two false assumptions.

I have quoted more of my letter than is relevant to the immediate question, because I think it shows something of my debt to Nock, the pressure under which I was working, the exhilaration of the work, and the way in which several quite different lines of

---

7. Professor J. Notopoulos, of Hartford. The references are to M. Parry, "Studies in the Epic Technique of Oral Verse-Making, I: Homer and Homeric Style," *Harvard Studies in Classical Philology* 41(1930)73–147, and A. Lord, *The Singer of Tales,* Cambridge, Mass., 1960.

research had to be carried on simultaneously. Such clarity as this presentation may have results not from the original study, but from the subsequent sorting out of snatches of work, now on one question, now on another, subject to constant interruptions in a world where everything takes longer than one expects.

Following up Richardson's insights, I was able to modify some points, add some others, and support the whole with a great deal of evidence from early Christian writers. The results are such that I don't think there should be (though I don't doubt there will be) much dispute from now on about the facts that Mk. 10.13–45 was put together to accompany or explain an early Christian baptismal service, and that the secret material fits this purpose perfectly.

The most important modifications of Richardson's theory (and of my first impressions as given above) were as follows:

1. The whole section—secret Gospel and all—was intended to be understood as dealing, not with two rich youths, but with one. The one whom Jesus loves and who rejects him in Mk. 10.20–22 is identified with the one whom Jesus raises from the dead and who then loves and follows him in the secret Gospel. The moral symbolism is obvious and the identification has been made in Mark's regular fashion, by the use of identical phrases. Here there are two such phrases: First, "Looking at him, loved him" has been added to Mk. 10.21, where it makes no sense (as inspection of the text will show: if Jesus had not loved him would he have refused to answer his question and let him be damned? Or, because he loved him, did he lay on him this heavier requirement which he would not meet? The phrase evidently comes from the secret Gospel where it expresses the youth's natural response to his saviour. Its only function in 10.21 is to identify the two youths.) Second, "For he had many possessions" in Mk. 10.22 seems to have been repeated in the secret Gospel of which the present text, "for he was rich," is probably a scribal abbreviation due to the influence of Lk. 18.23.

2. Richardson's insight, that the nocturnal initiation in the secret Gospel was a baptism, not only is confirmed by the details of the story—the six days' preparation, the nocturnal setting, the sheet over the naked body—but also has a most important consequence: it effectively defines "the mystery of the kingdom of God" as a phrase referring to the baptismal rite.

3. The resurrection and initiation stories are so important for the baptismal purpose of the whole section that it seems they must have been originally part of it. Thus the content of the secret Gospel turns out to support the conclusion reached from the study of its relation to John: this material was part of an early document that Mark used; Mark rewrote it, but essentially it is older than Mark.

Before trying to square this with the results of the stylistic study, one more piece of evidence has to be taken into account: Clement's second quotation from the secret Gospel, the quotation he located after Mk. 10.46. Mark says, "And *they* come into Jericho." According to Clement, the secret Gospel goes on, "And the sister of the youth whom Jesus loved and his mother and Salome were there, and Jesus did not receive them." Then Mark continues, "And when *he* was leaving Jericho" . . .

It is clear that something has been cut out of Mark at this place, but was it what Clement says it was? The little story he quotes is wholly unlike any other New Testament tale. It has no point, no miracle, no saying, no use *except* to discredit Salome (the one person named) and her female associates. Moreover, the Greek verb meaning "receive" is one used in the New Testament only by Luke (both in his Gospel and in Acts); it stands out from the Markan vocabulary of the secret Gospel like a sore thumb; and it is used in a late, disciplinary sense—"approve of," almost "accept as communicants"—which it does not have in Luke-Acts, but does have in Clement's work. The supposition that it comes from Clement is plausible, especially because there is no difficulty in explaining why Clement cut off the rest of this story and substituted his own brief phrase.

The story was going to tell of a conversation between Jesus and Salome, but Salome, in early Christian literature, was a very shady lady.[8] Matthew, Luke, and John all deleted her name from their Gospels. All sorts of heretics, but worst of all the Carpocratians, appealed to her as an authority. We have one story that she tempted Jesus (how, is not told), another that she inquired about his getting onto her bed—a sufficient reason for inquiry, no doubt, but also a sufficient reason for Clement's cutting her conversation with Jesus out of the secret Gospel.

Hence it seems likely that the text of Mark has been mutilated at 10.46. This strengthens the preceding evidence that the secret Gospel was part of the original material and that our present text of Mark was produced by abbreviation, not expansion.

In that case, what becomes of the stylistic evidence which seemed to indicate that the new passages were imitations and expansions of Mark? Several answers are possible:

1. A number of details suggested that the common source of Mark and John was in Aramaic. If it was, then parts of it may have been translated first for use in an elementary Gospel for new converts (canonical Mark), while the secret teaching of the church continued in Aramaic. Later on, when the church became more hellenized, the secret passages would also have been translated. In this event the second translator might understandably have tried to imitate the style of the previous translation.

2. The longer of the passages quoted from the secret Gospel is the one on which the stylistic conclusions are mostly built. But this passage seems to have been the central text for one of the most important rituals of Mark's church. If so, it would have exercised a

8. This one should not be confused with the Herodian princess celebrated by Oscar Wilde. The name was common.

much greater influence than would ordinary sections of the Gospel, and the number of parallels to it would of course be greater.

3. The sections available for stylistic analysis are short and may be nontypical, so any conclusions built on them are insecure and cannot stand against the stronger arguments from the content.

With these suggestions I left the problem. First of all, I didn't think further research would much advance the question. Second, the question seemed one I could bypass. Even if the secret Gospel passages were expansions of Mark, they were expansions made very early, in the style and by the school of the original author; they must have had the same tradition behind them. Whether they were written down fifteen years earlier or ten years later would not make great difference to their historical value. For historical purposes, the important question was the nature of the tradition they represented. Why the secrecy? Why should baptism have been a secret rite? What did this shady tradition have to do with Jesus?

9

The Secret Tradition: Introduction

In the two preceding chapters there has been a good deal of jumping back and forth in time during the years between 1960 and 1963. This was not to be avoided if the results of the study were to be presented in logical order. Logically one question is prior to another, the answer of the first has to be found before you can attack the second, and so on. But actually, trying to study a text is like trying to untangle half a dozen snarled fishing lines. You start with any loose ends you can find and work wherever something seems to give. One day you get an idea about one question, another day about another. The massive drudgery of checking on the language of the letter and the Gospel had not kept me from thinking about the problems they raised, and particularly about the most interesting of those problems: the implications of the new Gospel. All sorts of ideas occurred to me. As they occurred I made notes of them, dropped the notes into a big envelope, and went on with my word counts. When the stylistic commentary on the Gospel was finished, I finally emptied the envelope and went through its contents.

I was amused to see how many times I had thought the same thing, and each time with the enthusiasm that accompanies an original idea. Many compare the human mind to a computer, but I fear it is more like a tape recorder. This makes the question of what you put in so important; the first step toward higher learning is to limit your intake.

After repetition, the most amusing trait of the material was self-contradiction. My ambivalence about the letter had not ended with my decision to edit it. For a long time I had cast about, trying to find plausible reasons for assigning both letter and Gospel to the middle ages, the Renaissance, or the seventeenth century. Thus a lot of the earlier slips in the envelope were covered with implausible conjectures. These I quietly dropped in the waste basket. An embarrassing number of ordinary stupidities followed them; to review such an intellectual diary is a short cut to momentary humility.

When the weeding was done, I had half a dozen piles of slips, each pile containing notes on one idea or complex of ideas.

The central problem, I had gradually come to see, was the element of secrecy in primitive Christian tradition. Why did Clement's church have a secret Gospel? And why did even this secret Gospel merely hint at further secrets it would not reveal (for instance, the content of "the mystery of the kingdom of God")? What was there to conceal?

A good way to attack any historical problem is to locate it in time and space. The main outlines of occidental history are pretty well known; so are the main characteristics of the occidental countries and cultures. Therefore, if you can place your problem in a given country at a given time, the history and characteristics of that country and time will both suggest the likely answers and give you a set of limits within which any possible answer must fall. In this case the problem was secrecy, so my first pile of slips dealt with secrecy in the ancient world generally, and particularly with secrecy in ancient Jerusalem.

Next to this there was a big pile on secrecy in the New Testament. The synoptic Gospels are full of it. John swarms with contradictions that look like deliberate riddles; both John and Luke hint at secret teaching to be given by the resurrected Jesus or by the spirit, after Jesus' death. Other cards recalled to my attention the secrecy of Paul, who boasts that he spoke in a mystery the wisdom of God which his Corinthian converts were not worthy to hear. Notes on the opposition between elementary and secret teaching in the Epistle to the Hebrews, on the new revelation of God's secrets in the Apocalypse, and so on, also went in this pile.

What most concerned me was the secrecy of Jesus and particularly "the mystery of the kingdom of God," since that phrase appeared in the text. Much of Jesus' secretiveness seemed to be tied up with his role as Messiah, and the Messiah was certainly connected with the kingdom. But just what did Jesus have to do with it? What kind of a Messiah was he? This was a famous subject of dispute. Somewhere along the line, I don't remember just where, it had occurred to me that a good way to define Jesus' role would be to compare him with John the Baptist. What could he do that the Baptist couldn't? Consequently I had done a good deal of thinking about the Baptist and a whole pile of slips dealt with him.

The Baptist stood on one side of Jesus; on the other stood Paul. Jesus might be defined as the middle term between them—and a short middle term, at that. According to all reports, his ministry began soon after his baptism and lasted, at most, about three years. Paul's conversion, according to his own account in Galatians, must have occurred within four or five years of the crucifixion, perhaps less. So not more than eight years, and probably less, separated Paul from the Baptist. Why not, then, compare the Baptist with Paul, determine the differences, and try to see how many of these could be traced back to Jesus? This idea must have occurred fairly early—it had produced a big pile of notes and an even bigger bibliography.

The obvious point for comparison between the Baptist and Paul was their practice of baptism. Three peculiarities of Paul's practice had particularly caught my attention: it was the work of the spirit;

it united the recipient with Jesus, his death, burial, resurrection, and ascent into the heavens; and it set men free from the law. On each of these points I had accumulated some material. Most of the parallels seemed to come from magical texts; it was clear that I'd have to do more research on that side of the subject.

Ascent into the heavens brought back memories of my work on the *hekalot* books, to which I now returned.[1] They, too, had been a secret literature. But even more important as a possible explanation of secrecy was the notion of liberty from the law. There had evidently been a powerful and long-lived libertine tradition in early Christianity; the literature was full of hostile references to it. Most of it had been more or less secret. Here was another subject on which in 1962 I found some notes in my envelope, but saw I had a great deal more to do. Another reason for tracking down libertinism was that the secret Gospel had been used by the Carpocratians as well as the orthodox, and the Carpocratians were among the later and more notorious representatives of the libertine tradition.

All the above—secrecy in general, in the teaching of Jesus, and in the New Testament, Jesus' relation to the kingdom of God and to the Baptist, Pauline baptism and the magical background of its peculiarities, the libertine tradition and the Carpocratians—all these subjects, I could see, were directly relevant to my problem. Each one would have to be studied in detail to determine just what information it would yield.

That was the state of the question in the fall of 1962, when I had just finished my work on the style of the Gospel. The problem of its relation in content to John and the synoptics still lay ahead. I had scarcely touched another question: the history of the text. (How did the secret Gospel disappear? Why do we never hear of

1. See my "Observations on *Hekhalot Rabbati*," in *Biblical and Other Studies*, ed. A. Altmann, Harvard University Press, 1963 (Lown Institute, *Studies and Texts*, vol. I) pp. 142–160.

it? How did Clement's letter get to Mar Saba? What became of
the manuscript from which the present copy was made?) And I
was determined to get the whole job off my hands by the summer
of 1963, when I had a sabbatical year coming. July 1963 would
see the fifth anniversary of the discovery, and after five years of
intensive study of the text I had better have a change. Work at a
problem too long and you find yourself unable to see anything but
the arguments you have already seen. So in the fall of 1962 I had
only eight months left.

I did what I could. The work on the Gospel text and content—
as distinct from the tradition—was completed. For the tradition,
I put together in a sketch the material of my notes and the results
of such research as I managed to do. It was clear that the relation
of the tradition to magic required much more investigation. To
that I decided to devote my sabbatical year. Grants from the
American Council of Learned Societies and the Bollingen Foundation enabled me to plan a trip by land around the Mediterranean,
to visit the local museums and hunt for magical material. In the
last months of the spring term of 1963 I did the research on the
history of the text, and then came the time for the take-off. That
chapter was written in Rome, and the first draft was done.

Eight months later, after much travel and work on other problems, I revised the draft from end to end. The revised version was
accepted for publication by the Harvard University Press. I wanted
a further revision—my work on magic was yielding a wealth of
new material. So the final text was not ready until August 1966.
Since then it has been "going through the press." I have reread
it a couple of times and made minor changes, but no more.
Reference works and similar compilations of data can and should
be brought up to date, but a work of interpretive scholarship is an
account of intuitions and arguments, a picture of a given problem
as seen by a given person at a given time. When it is finished it is

finished, for better or for worse. To quote a distinguished Roman administrator, "What I have written, I have written."

The following text, accordingly, is a summary of my findings, substantially as worked out in 1966, on the secret tradition in early Christianity. The problem is so complex and my thoughts about it moved along so many different lines that there is no possibility of setting out the discoveries in something like chronological order, as I have tried to do in the preceding chapters. Here I shall have to follow the intellectual structure of the argument.

10

The Mystery and the Kingdom

The most important thing in the new text was the initiation
story:

And going out of the tomb they came into the house of the youth,
for he was rich. And after six days Jesus told him what to do, and in
the evening the youth comes to him, wearing a linen cloth over his
naked body. And he remained with him that night, for Jesus taught
him the mystery of the kingdom of God.

What was this mystery of the kingdom of God, and why should
it be taught secretly, in a nocturnal initiation? These were the
primary questions that had to be answered. If I could find an
answer for these, it would probably solve the secondary problems:
Why were parts of Mark's Gospel kept secret? Why was baptism
a secret rite? What was the secret tradition in early Christianity?

There were some clues in Mark. In chapter 4 he told about
Jesus teaching the crowds in "parables," that is, in stories of which
the reference was not clear. When the crowds had gone, Jesus'
closer followers asked him about the parables. "And he said to
them, 'To you the mystery of the kingdom of God has been given,
but to those outside everything is in parables, so that they may see,
indeed, but not perceive, and hear, indeed, but not understand,

lest they should repent and be forgiven' " (Mk. 4.11f). After this he went on to explain the parables he had used.

Matthew and Luke, when reworking Mark, identified the mystery with the explanations of the parables, so they changed Jesus' answer and made him say, "To you it has been given *to know* the *mysteries* of the kingdom," i.e., the following explanations. But this was not what Mark had said. For him "the [single] mystery" was something that already *had been* given to the disciples; the fact that they had already received it made them different from "those outside" and fit to hear the explanations. Matthew and Luke may have misunderstood this, or they may have changed the text in order to conceal the reference to the mystery.

What, then, was the mystery? The secret Gospel now gives us a glimpse of it. It was something that was "taught" by night to a disciple who came "after six days," "wearing a linen cloth over his naked body." The six days' preparation, the linen sheet and the nudity, but most of all the context of this story in Mark, indicate that the mystery was a baptism. If so, the word "taught" is strange. In the ancient world mystery rites like baptism were generally said to be "given" to the initiates. Perhaps the secret Gospel originally had "gave" and some copyist, influenced by his memories of Matthew and Luke, changed it to "taught." (The two words, in Greek, are somewhat similar, and such corruptions of Gospel texts by recollections of parallel passages from other Gospels are very common.)

Now that we have the secret Gospel we can also understand a passage in the canonical Gospel of Mark that hitherto has been an insoluble puzzle in a fantastic frame. Mark's story of Jesus' last day of liberty and his arrest (Mk. 14.12–52) reads like something from the adventures of a revolutionist. According to him, Jesus had created some sort of disturbance in the Jerusalem temple and the high priests, who were also the city authorities, were wait-

ing for a chance to arrest him privately, when the arrest would not
be likely to cause a riot. He therefore came into the city only by
day, with the crowds, and spent the nights in a village near the
desert, from which he could escape if any troops were seen coming. But for the Passover he had to spend at least the evening in
Jerusalem. Evidently he was in touch with some friends there, but
did not wholly trust his disciples. (The distrust was well grounded;
one of them did, in fact, betray him.) When he sent a couple of
disciples to make preparations for the Passover meal, he did not
tell them the address, but told them to look for a man carrying a
pitcher of water. (Carrying water was women's work, so this was
like saying, "Look for a man wearing lipstick.") They followed
the water carrier and where he went in they gave a prearranged
message to the owner of the house, who then showed them an
upper room in which they prepared the meal.

Jesus came at evening "with the twelve." After the meal and
the mysterious communion ritual that accompanied it, they went
out of the city to the foot of the Mount of Olives, where there is
a stream. There Jesus told most of the disciples to wait for him.
He went on some distance farther with only Peter, James, and
John. Then he told them also to wait and keep watch, and went
on yet farther by himself. According to Mark, he had often pre-
dicted that he would be betrayed, arrested, handed over to the
Romans, and crucified. It is not unlikely that he had occasionally,
in pessimistic moments, expressed such forebodings. But the fact
that he set guards indicates that on this particular evening he had
no intention of being arrested if he could help it. So the story of
his prayers—the famous "agony in the garden"—that Mark puts
in here (14.35–42) is probably pure invention. Mark says the
disciples were asleep at the time; if so, who provided his information? They woke up just as the police arrived. Some of them put
up a short fight, but to no avail. They ran, Jesus was arrested.
"And with him there was a young man wearing a linen cloth over

[his] naked [body], and they grab him, but he left the cloth and got away naked" (Mk. 14.51f.).

Through seventeen hundred years of New Testament scholarship, nobody has ever been able to explain what that young man was doing alone with Jesus in such a place, at such a time, and in such a costume. All too serious scholars have been reduced to suggesting that the youth was an innocent bystander, walking in his sleep. The secret Gospel, however, gives the clue. The business in hand was a baptism; the youth wore the required costume. The time—night—agrees with the story in the secret gospel; the place —beside a stream in a lonely garden—is suitable. The preceding secrecy has obvious prudential explanations. The communion ceremony at the meal may have been an attempt by Jesus to bind his disciples to himself in such a way as to prevent betrayal. To that question we shall come back later.

This was all I could get out of Mark and the secret Gospel: Jesus had a "mystery of the kingdom of God," a baptismal rite, which he administered to some, at least, of his disciples. It was nocturnal, secret, and Mark thought it required six days' preparation.

So I came back again to the questions, What was all this secrecy about? Why should Jesus' baptismal rite have been secret when the Baptist's had been public? And behind these questions lay others: Was Mark's report true? Did Jesus really have such a secret practice, or was Mark merely attributing to him a usage grown up in the early churches? These latter questions, I saw, would have to wait. The first problem was to find out the secret.

What sorts of secrets were there in the Greco-Roman world? When I started to look, I found them everywhere. Children of course had them and loved them—they still do. To have a secret is the beginning of independence, consequently much of the world of children is jealously closed off from adult observation. In this respect, as in many, adults are big children, so the adult world, too, was and is full of secrets. At one end of the social scale in antiquity were the *arcana imperii,* the secrets of the imperial government known only to the emperor and his confidential ministers. At the other were the secret societies of the slaves whose members made themselves known to each other by inconspicuous signs and passwords. Above the slaves came the women, and the world of women, then as now, was largely a secret world to which few men had access. But even within the world of free men secrecy was on every side—in politics, in business organizations, in the handicrafts and the professions. The secrets of the medical profession are still guarded by the ancient "Hippocratic" oath: "I swear by Apollo the Healer . . . that I will teach this art . . to my sons and to the sons of him who taught me, and to the pupils who have been enrolled by contract and sworn by the physicians' oath, *and to none other.* . . . Whatever in medical practice, or even outside practice, I either see or hear . . . which ought not be told to outsiders, I shall keep secret." Every philosophic school had its secret doctrines; most schools were closed to outsiders; some even had underground meeting places. Religion was yet more secretive than philosophy. There were innumerable "mystery" cults of which the initiates were sworn not to reveal the rites. Most of these were local, but some were empire-wide and counted their communities by the hundreds. And beyond religion was magic, which was practiced secretly everywhere by persons on every level of society.

Within this secretive world, Judaism was at home. Its official centers, down to A.D. 70, were two temples, one in Jerusalem, the other in Egypt. In these only the high priest might enter the central room, only the hereditary priests might come near it, and only Jews might even enter the main courtyard. Outside the temples, the Jews were cut off from their neighbors by purity laws which, if strictly interpreted, forbade them to enter a gentile's house or receive a gentile in their own houses, let alone eat with one. To touch a gentile, or his clothing, or any object he had sat or lain on, made one impure. Consequently many Jews kept to themselves; relatively few gentiles knew much of what went on inside a synagogue, not to speak of the legendary temples; and Judaism was generally classed as a "mystery religion." The Jews themselves represented it as such and described circumcision and the passover meal as "mysteries."

Many Jews did not observe the purity laws strictly. Of those who did, however, different groups interpreted them differently and therefore thought each other's members unclean. And all the strict observants—Pharisees, Sadducees, Essenes, and so on—thought ordinary Jews unclean. Hence their meals, their houses, their schools, and their synagogues were generally closed not only to gentiles, but to ordinary Jews and to members of the competing sects. Some groups in early Christianity followed much the same practices. Thus Mark made Jesus distinguish between his baptized followers, to whom the mystery had been given, and "those outside"—everybody else. The outsiders were not to be told the secrets of the sect. The same use of "outsiders" is found in Jewish sectarian (Pharisaic) material.

Groups cut off from the outside world by such legal barriers usually developed further peculiarities of doctrine and practice. Among these was apt to be a deliberate affectation of secrecy about their teachings and rites. This resulted partly from the childish delight in having secrets. Partly, too, it seems to have been an imitation of the practices of the philosophic schools and the mystery cults. Other groups were involved in revolutionary activities or had magical or libertine practices that gave them serious reasons for secrecy.

In the sectarian center at Qumran by the Dead Sea, where magic was practiced and revolution anticipated, it was a legal obligation to conceal from outsiders the true meaning of the Mosaic law. Before any outsider could be taught the rules of the sect he had to undergo an examination and take an oath to keep the teachings

secret. Then there were two years of probation before he was admitted. And even then he was not in the inner circle. The group
had some documents written in outlandish alphabets which were
evidently used to keep the contents secret from ordinary members.
One of the secrets thus concealed was probably the technique of
self-hypnosis that was believed to enable the magician to ascend
into the heavens and deal directly with the angels. This later produced the *hekalot* books, which were originally secret. Fragments
from similiar works have been found at Qumran. We are told that
the names of the angels (certainly used for "practical" purposes,
i.e., magic) were among the most valued secrets of the Essenes.

The secrecy of the Qumran sect was not at all unique. The
priests of the Jerusalem temple had a large body of secret traditions and practices. So did the priests of the Samaritans, just to the
north of Jerusalem, and among the Samaritans, as among the Jews,
there were a number of secret sects.

The Jewish sect we know best, the Pharisees, had secret doctrines about God, his name, his throne, the heavens, creation, the
structure of the world, the coming End, the reasons for the law,
sexual questions, magical formulae, discreditable traditions, and
laws likely to be abused. And these were only the matters that
were kept secret *within* the group, from its own less reliable members. In relation to outsiders—and that means, to ordinary Jews,
not to mention gentiles—the whole Pharisaic sect was an esoteric
group. Public teaching was normally prohibited. And even when
outsiders asked questions, they might not be given the correct answers. We have stories of rabbis who gave obscure answers and
then explained the true ones in private to their disciples. Exactly
similar stories are told of Jesus (Mk. 4.10ff; 7.17ff; 10.10ff;
13.3ff). Clement in his letter told Theodore to act on the same
principle: "Not all true things are to be said to all men."

Such stories about Jesus offended some liberal critics of the
eighteenth and nineteenth centuries, who therefore declared them

false. Mark, they said, was using this device to put into Jesus' mouth things he wished Jesus had said. These things were not in the tradition, so he could not pass them off as Jesus' public teaching. Therefore he pretended that Jesus had taught them privately.

This theory leads to serious difficulties. Can we suppose that when Mark was written, forty or fifty years after Jesus' death, the Christians it was written for (in Rome?) were so well acquainted with *all* of Jesus' teachings that the author would have had to use this device to sneak in some new ones? Not likely. Besides, if they *had* been so well informed about details, they would certainly have known whether or not Jesus had taught in secret. If he had not, there would have been no possibility of passing off stories about his secret teaching. So the existence of such stories in Mark, our earliest Gospel, would presuppose an even earlier tradition that Jesus in fact did teach in secret. All the Gospels represent him as doing so.[1] Had he not done so, he would have been a unique exception among the religious teachers of his time.

Actually the reports of Jesus' secret practices are not limited to these few stories. They are all over the Gospels. We are often told that before performing a cure he took the sick man aside, privately. Or, if he went in where the patient was, he shut out everyone and took with him only his closest disciples. After his miracles he repeatedly ordered the persons concerned to keep the event secret. He also kept his movements secret, so that even the people following him did not know where he had gone, or where he came from, when he reappeared. He would go off by himself or with his closest disciples, and nobody knew what happened. It was said that his disciples sometimes saw him in a different form, talking with supernatural beings, but this, too, he told them to keep secret. Important men came to see him by night; some were said to be his

1. The statement in Jn. 18.20, "I have said nothing in secret," is an apologetic claim made in a trial. It is contradicted by John himself (19.38; ch. 3 entire; etc.) and by many stories and sayings in the synoptics.

disciples, but in secret. When he did teach in public, he taught in parables and cryptic sayings. Who could know just what they meant? Even his disciples are said to have misunderstood and to have asked him privately for explanations.

All these traits are well known. For the past hundred years they have been discussed again and again. The common explanation offered for them is that Jesus thought he was the Messiah, the servant of God expected to come, overthrow the Romans, and establish a Jewish kingdom that would rule the world. The Romans took a dim view of such expectations and discouraged them by killing all the messianic pretenders they could catch. Consequently when Jesus' disciples began to think him the Messiah, he had an excellent reason for warning them to keep the fact a secret. Many scholars supposed his secret movements, obscure teaching, and so on were all to be explained as attempts to avoid the authorities and to prevent any popular excitement that might attract the authorities' attention.

This explanation is based on Mark and is probably true, but incomplete. Of course it has embarrassed Christian scholars who have therefore produced a number of modifications. Some have said that Jesus did not share the ordinary messianic expectations. He looked for a purely spiritual kingdom, not of the Jews, but of all men. The Jews would not tolerate such a teaching, so he had to keep it secret. Others have said that he didn't think he was the Messiah at all. He was merely a protestant preacher who expressed himself so badly that his disciples produced this whole structure of misunderstandings. Such theories need not detain us.

The real objection to the common interpretation of the "messianic secret" is that it does not suffice to explain *all* the secrecy. And there is no reason to think that Jesus had only one secret. The stories told about him suggest he had many. Why, when he cured demoniacs, did he try to prevent them from speaking? Why the secrecy about his other cures? What about the secret communion meal and the mystery of the kingdom of God that he gave to his followers? Of course these are all connected with Jesus' belief that he was the Messiah, but they indicate that there was something peculiar about that belief. There were secrets behind the messianic secret, and they seem to have concerned the nature of "the kingdom of God."

About "the kingdom of God" most scholars are in agreement. It means primarily "the rule of God," but it can also refer by extension to the persons or areas ruled. At Jesus' time many Palestinian Jews believed that originally the kingdom had included all creation, but since the time of Adam certain provinces had been in revolt. Not only men, but some of the angels were disobedient, and the disobedient angels had seized control of much of the earth. But this state of affairs was not going to last. Soon God, like a Roman emperor, would come with his armies to restore his rule. His enemies would either be killed or brought before him for judgment. At that time his friends, too, would get their rewards.

From this common belief Jesus' followers differed by thinking that the suppression of the revolt had already begun with the coming of Jesus as God's representative. God's rule, his "kingdom," was now present again in the lower world. It had come in Jesus' person; it was manifested in his acts of power; it was extended by his disciples' obedience; it was organized in their churches; and it would be completed when Jesus came back at the head of the angelic armies "with power and great glory to judge both the living and the dead." This explains why the New Testament books generally speak of the kingdom both as present and as future. It was both at once. It was present in Jesus, in the Church, and in God's eternal rule of the heavens; it was yet to come in the full resubjugation of the lower world.

Particularly important for our purpose is the presence of the kingdom in God's rule of the heavens, which were thought to be a number of spherical bodies, concentric with the earth and surrounding it, one outside another. God lived in the "highest"— the outermost—of these spheres. There was his throne; there were the greatest of the unfallen angels. The spheres had gates in them, giving passage from one to another. These were the gates of the kingdom of the heavens; their keys were the keys of the kingdom. The New Testament passages about entering the kingdom commonly refer to entering the heavens. Abraham was up there; a poor man was carried to him by angels, immediately after death. There was the paradise to which Paul was taken up, to which four second-century rabbis ascended, and to which Jesus went after his crucifixion. (He promised to take along, that same day, the penitent thief who was being crucified with him.) There, too, was the reward promised to the righteous, the kingdom prepared for them from the beginning of creation.[2] There God's will was always done, as the Church still prays it may, in the future, be done on earth; there God always maintained the peace that the Synagogue still prays for.[3]

Thus "the kingdom of God" had many different meanings—God's rule in general, its expression in his acts of power and in men's obedience, the organization of those who obey him (the Church), the area in which his rule is now unquestioned (the heavens), the coming restoration of his rule over the lower world. Consequently "the mystery of the kingdom of God" had many possible meanings. Which sense of "the kingdom" should be understood?

Since Jesus could give "the mystery of the kingdom" to his disciples, the sense in which "kingdom" was used in that expression would probably be clear if I could find out what Jesus had to do with the kingdom. And it was my hunch that I could find this out by comparing Jesus with John the Baptist.

2. Mt. 5.12; 8.11; Lk. 6.23; 12.32f; 13.28; 16.22f; 23.42f; II Cor. 12.1–4; II Tim. 4.18. *The Jerusalem Talmud, Hagigah* II.1(77b).

3. The prayers referred to are "the Lord's prayer" (Mt. 6.9–13) and the terminal blessing, "May he who makes peace in his heavens make peace for us and for all Israel."

11

Jesus' Relation to the Kingdom

John the Baptist was an important man. He was a preacher of
repentance who attracted an enormous following and set off violent
disputes. The rulers of his time were offended by his moral criticism
and frightened by the thought that he might become the leader of
a revolutionary movement. All Judea, Jerusalem, and Transjordan
went out to him, in crowds. Masses of the common people accepted
his teaching and received his baptism. The authorities of the Jerusalem temple were afraid to speak against him, even after his
death, because of his popular following. When he was finally arrested and executed many believed that God would punish the
crime. The defeat of a Jewish army shortly thereafter was thought
to be part of the punishment. Some of his disciples were sure he
was the Messiah; they carried his sect as far as Egypt and Asia
Minor. His career is reported by the Jewish historian Josephus as
well as by the Gospels; attacks on him or his followers appear in
the Gospels, the Book of Acts, and the Qumran documents.

Besides all this, he started Christianity—a detail that probably
went almost unnoticed in his lifetime. He did so by baptizing
Jesus, who had some sort of ecstatic experience after the baptism.
This event was remembered by Christian writers as "the beginning
of the Gospel" (Mk. 1.1ff and parallels; Jn. 1.6). The story would
seem to have come ultimately from Jesus himself—who else would

have known? It is supported by the fact that Christian traditions repeatedly refer to this as the point from which the movement began. "The law and the prophets were until John." "From then on" is the Christian period (Lk. 16.16; Mt. 11.12f; cf. Acts 1.22; 10.37; 13.23f).

By good luck, we know the reason for the Baptist's importance. He was not just a preacher of repentance who backed up his preachment by the (false) warning that the End was at hand, God was about to restore his kingdom on earth. Prophets had been preaching that message for the past eight hundred years and the repeated failure of their prophecies had done a good deal to discredit it. It had no novelty and probably would not have had much success— by itself. But the Baptist added a new element. He proclaimed that there was something his hearers could *do* to prepare for the coming of the kingdom, something easy, cheap, and not very unpleasant. They could be "baptized"—immersed in water—and so get rid of all their past sins and start a new life with a clean slate. This "baptism for the remission of sins" was the new thing that John preached; it made him "more than a prophet" (Mt. 11.9ff; Lk. 7.26ff) and got him the nickname by which he is still remembered, "the Baptist."

All over the world, from very early times, men have tried to wash off spiritual pollution as if it were physical dirt. In ancient Israel, however, this practice had been specialized for getting rid of ritual impurity, as opposed to sins. "Ritual impurity" is a sort of pollution supposed to attach to a man if he touches, no matter how slightly, a dead body or the impure secretions of a living body, or something of the sort. Essentially it has nothing to do either with dirt or with sin. The Old Testament paid no attention to dirt, prescribed immersions to get rid of ritual impurity, but ruled that nothing could atone for sin except sacrifices and repentance.[1] By

---

1. In a few poetic passages, prophets and psalmists talked about sins as if they were impurities, but this metaphorical usage had no effect on the law.

John's time the only place in Palestine where a Jew could legally sacrifice was the Jerusalem temple. The temple priesthood had a valuable monopoly and made the most of it; Jesus called the place a robbers' cave. Besides, if a man lived a distance from Jerusalem, the cost of travel might be even greater than that of sacrificing. So when John introduced a new way to get rid of sins, a simple, inexpensive rite that could be performed anywhere, the indignation of the priests at this cut-rate competition, and the enthusiasm of the common people, can be imagined.

The Gospels tell us the Baptist got his rite "from God" (Mk. 11.30ff). That is to say, it was an "inspiration"—his own idea—and he introduced it by his authority as a prophet (Mt. 11.9 and parallels). This, he believed, was what God had sent him to do. His function was to prepare men for the coming of the kingdom not only by warning them of it and urging them to repent, but also by administering this new ritual to cleanse them of their sins and make them ready to meet their God. His baptism was not something one could do for oneself; it had to be done by the Baptist or one of his disciples. It seems to have been public, was administered to Jews (whether or not to gentiles), either required or effected repentance, was accompanied by confession of sins, effected remission of sins, required the performance of good works in the future, and was not expected to "give the spirit," that is, to produce any hallucinations or violent and sudden reactions in the recipient. There is no evidence that all those whom John baptized became his disciples, or members of any sort of society. The stories of crowds coming to be baptized, and the absence of any reference to any sizable society, combine to suggest that the baptized did not form an organization. What was demanded of the few who did become his disciples, we don't know.

Nothing like this seems to have been known in Judaism before the Baptist's time. In spite of common statements to the contrary, there was nothing like it at Qumran; the Essenes had special im-

mersions, but only for purity; the *Manual of Discipline* goes out
of its way to insist that no amount of physical washing can remove
sin. The Pharisees later developed a practice of immersing *gentiles*
when they became converts to Judaism. This rite may have been
influenced by the Baptist's, or by early Christian baptism, or both;
but it has important differences from both and cannot possibly have
been the source of either. So the Baptist's rite was probably all his
own. It defined his peculiar role in relation to the kingdom. He
was not merely a prophet. He was "the forerunner," the one sent
to prepare for the coming of the King, not merely to announce it,
but to purify the people and make them ready by his peculiar rite.

Since the role of the Baptist in relation to the kingdom is so
clearly definable, why is the role of Jesus so obscure? The Gospels
say that he was the Messiah and they expect him to be the chief
executive in the future, when the kingdom comes "with power."
But his function in his own time is not clearly distinguished. He is
generally represented as an advance agent, sent to proclaim the
coming of the kingdom and to exemplify its presence, to manifest
its power in his miracles and its requirements in his preaching. But
all this could have been done by any prophet, let alone by the
Baptist, who was "more than a prophet." So what did Jesus' followers think that he could do, but the Baptist couldn't?

It does no good to say that for the Baptist the kingdom was yet
to come, in Jesus' work it was present. If the kingdom is simply
the rule of God, it is present whenever God manifests his power
and men obey him. So if the presence of the kingdom means only
its presence in preaching and prediction and acts of power, it had
already been present in the work of the prophets. But on the one
hand, the Gospels insist that Jesus, like the Baptist, was more than
a prophet;[2] on the other, they do not represent him as a penitent
nor, *usually,* as a preacher of repentance, and they contain no accounts of mass repentance, and few of individuals' repentance,

2. Mk. 8.28f and parallels; Mt. 11.9ff; Lk. 7.26ff; Jn. 4.19–26; 7.40ff; etc.

produced by his preaching. No doubt Jesus did preach repentance occasionally; most preachers do. But to judge from the Gospels it was not a major theme in his teaching, and there is no reason to suppose that the Gospels would have concealed it if it had been— in fact, they often seem to have increased it.

Further, the Baptist, who certainly did preach repentance, conducted himself accordingly: he wore nothing but an old piece of haircloth and a leather belt, he lived in the desert, and ate next to nothing. Jesus came "eating and drinking" and his enemies called him a pig and a drunk (Mt. 11.19; Lk. 7.34). The followers of the Baptist and those of the Pharisees fasted; Jesus' followers did not, and Jesus justified this by comparing them to the members of a bridal party. He justified their laxity (and his own) in observance of the law by comparing them to the companions of David (this made him the new David—the Messiah). He forgave sin freely, often without demanding repentance. He blessed, not the fasting, but the hungry, and his blessing was that they should be filled.[3] Whatever else he may have been, he certainly was not a conventional prophet of doom and preacher of repentance. What, then, did he have to do with the kingdom?

Both Jesus and the Baptist were said to be more than prophets. We know why this was said of the Baptist—because of his introduction of "baptism for the remission of sins." So we should look for some similar rite that Jesus introduced. The secret Gospel told of such a rite, "the mystery of the kingdom of God," and the context of this in Mark showed that it must have been a baptism. But none of the synoptic Gospels ever said anything about Jesus' having baptized anybody. And the fourth Gospel contradicts itself on this point, as on many others. In 3.22 it says that he did baptize; in 3.26 and 4.1 it refers to reports of his baptizing; but in 4.2 it says, "Jesus himself did not baptize, but his disciples." In normal

---

3. Lk. 6.20f. The Lukan version of this saying is generally recognized to be more nearly original than that in Mt. 5.6ff.

Greek this would mean that Jesus himself did not baptize, but his disciples [did]. However, the Greek of the fourth Gospel is often abnormal, and this might be a bad translation of an Aramaic statement that Jesus baptized *nobody but* his disciples. And the statement in 3.22, that he did baptize, is clear. So the fourth Gospel probably supports the secret Gospel, while the silence of the synoptics can be explained by the fact that baptism was part of the secret teaching.

Historical probability also supports the secret Gospel. Jesus himself was baptized. Baptism seems to have been a crucial experience in his life. Why should he have rejected it? His followers were baptizing converts a few years after his death. If Jesus had rejected the rite, would they immediately have taken it up? The Baptist's great success had been due to his introduction of a new rite that prepared his followers for the kingdom and made them think him greater than the prophets. Would Jesus, a client of the Baptist and himself baptized, have gone back to the old prophetic routine of mere preaching? We come back again to the question, What was his special role in relation to the kingdom? He was the Messiah. So what? What was there that he, the Messiah, could *do,* now that he had come, which neither a prophet nor even the Baptist could do?

The Gospels give us the answer. He could admit his followers to the kingdom of God, and he could do it in some special way, so that they were not there merely by anticipation, nor by virtue of belief and obedience, nor by some other figure of speech, but were really, actually, in.

This was never claimed for any prophet, nor even for the Baptist. But there are lots of statements in the synoptics—and in all parts of them, from the earliest to the latest—that represent the kingdom as already, somehow, attainable, and the disciples as already in it. They are the members of the wedding party, who cannot be made to fast, who need not observe the sabbath nor the purity laws. The law and the prophets were until John, and until his time the lawyers hindered those who were entering the kingdom. But now the kingdom can be taken by violence; the mystery has been given to the disciples. If anyone knocks, it will be opened; whoever asks, receives. The kingdom is like a field with a hidden treasure, a secret pearl that can be purchased now. It is already here, growing like a mustard seed, spreading like leaven through dough. Peter, indeed, has the keys to the kingdom already, while he is here on earth. And all the twelve chosen disciples have power over demons, can heal the sick and even raise the dead. Whoever hears them, hears Jesus. The Father has been revealed to them by the Son. They have seen Jesus in his true glory, have eaten his flesh and drunk his blood. The least of those who is now in the kingdom is greater than the Baptist. The prodigal son has been admitted at once to the feast.[4]

Some of these elements are clearer and more convincing than others; the clear ones show how the others should be interpreted. Many different sorts and strata of material are represented; this shows that these notions are not a peculiarity of any one strand of the tradition. Their wide distribution indicates an early, common source. That source would also lie behind the present union of the disciples with Jesus in John (15.1ff). Paul, too, says the believers are already in the kingdom (Col. 1.13). So does the Apocalypse (1.6; etc.). Where did all this come from, if not from Jesus? It seems that somehow he enabled at least some of his followers to enter the kingdom at once and to enter it in some special way, presumably by some rite that would make them greater than the Baptist, exempt them from the law, and give them supernatural powers. This admission was the special function of Jesus the Messiah, the function that even the Baptist could not perform.

Now the recognized means of preparation for admission to the

4. Mk. 2.19,25ff; 3.15; 4.11,30f; 7.2ff; 9.2ff; 14.22ff; Lk. 7.28; 10.9,16f,22; 11.10,52; 13.21; 15.22ff; 16.16; 17.21; Mt. 11.28ff; 13.44ff; 16.19.

kingdom—recognized by Jesus himself, since he had used it—was baptism. And baptism became later the means of admission to the Church, the kingdom present on earth. Therefore Jesus probably admitted his chosen followers to the kingdom by some sort of baptism. *This was the mystery of the kingdom—the mystery rite by which the kingdom was entered.*

I don't remember how many false starts I made through the labyrinth before I found my way to this conclusion. But I still remember my relief at reaching it. Not that I was sure it was right. But it gave me a hypothesis, a theory to test, and half the battle in research is to find your theory.

In this case the theory had to take account of all the different elements reviewed in the past two chapters, and fit them together into a comprehensible pattern. This much the above hypothesis did. It also had to explain the secrecy about the baptism introduced by Jesus, and it did this, too. If his baptism admitted the recipients to the kingdom in some special way that gave them supernatural powers, put them beyond the law, and so on, then he might understandably have kept it secret and given it only to his chosen followers.

Alas, comprehensible patterns and understandable explanations are not always correct. If the first half of the battle is to find your theory, the second half is to test it. You must consider not only the problems it answers, but the problems it raises.

In this case, the most important problem raised was a question of fact: Is there any actual evidence—apart from what we have seen in Mark and the secret Gospel—for Jesus' practice of such a baptismal rite and for the nature of the rite he practiced?

Once this question was clear, I knew what I was looking for, and presently found it. Historians usually find what they are looking for—a fact that makes me uneasy. But anyhow, I saw what I think I see, and it amounts to substantial New Testament evidence for the existence and nature of Jesus' baptismal rite.

12

The Secret Baptism

The best evidence for the baptism Jesus administered (which, henceforth, I shall call "Jesus' baptism") comes from a comparison between the Baptist's baptism and that of Paul. Jesus' crucifixion probably occurred within three years after he was baptized, and Paul was probably baptized within two or three years of the crucifixion. Therefore what Paul was told when he was baptized will have been pretty close to Jesus' teaching, as that had been reinterpreted by his disciples after the crucifixion and their consequent visions. Paul certainly had a powerful and original mind, and he developed his own interpretation of baptism, as of most other aspects of Christianity. The interpretation he developed is what has come down to us, through passing references in letters written fifteen or twenty years after he was baptized. So we cannot take it, by any means, as mere report of Jesus' teaching, but we can reasonably suppose that the primary elements came from Jesus.

The main passages are four:

Rom. 6.3ff: Those of us who were baptized into Messiah Jesus were baptized into his death. That is to say, we were buried with him, through the baptism into death, in order that, just as Messiah was raised from the dead through the glory of the Father, thus we too should live a new life. For if we have been united with him by sharing his death, we shall be so, too, [by sharing his] resurrection. For we know that the man we once were was crucified with him, in order that the body which belonged to sin might be made ineffective, so that we should no longer be slaves to sin. For when a man dies he is no longer answerable for his sins. And if we died with Messiah, we believe that we shall also [continue to] live with him, knowing that Messiah, having been raised from the dead, will never again die.

I Cor. 12.12f: For just as the body is one, but has many members . . . so also is the Messiah. And thus we all were baptized with one spirit to [constitute] one body—whether Jews or Greeks, whether slaves or freemen—and we were all given one spirit to drink.

Gal. 3.26ff: For all of you [formerly gentiles] are sons of God through the faith in Messiah Jesus. For as many of you as were baptized into Messiah have been clothed with Messiah. In [him] there is neither Jew nor Greek, there is neither slave nor freeman, there is no male and female, for you all are one in Messiah Jesus. And if you are [parts] of Messiah, then you are [parts of] *the* [one] seed of Abraham and heirs according to the promise [made by God to Abraham about his *one* seed.]

Col. 2.9–3.4: [In the Messiah] all the fullness of the divine dwells bodily. And you are fulfilled in him, since he is the head of every [cosmic] power and authority. In him you have also been circumcised, not with [the] physical [image of] circumcision, [but] with the stripping off of the body of flesh, with the circumcision of the Messiah, having been buried with him in baptism, in which you have also been resurrected together [with him] through the faith in the working of God who raised him from the dead. Thus, when you were dead in your sins and in the foreskin of your flesh, [God] brought you to life together with him. Having forgiven us all our sins, he [the Messiah] has canceled the bond with the legal demands which was against us and has set it aside, having nailed it to the cross. Having stripped off the [cosmic] powers and authorities he has made a public spectacle of them and led them, by means of it [the cross], [as captives] in his triumphal procession. Therefore let no man sit in judgment on you about food and drink, or in a matter of festival or new moon or sabbaths, which are a shadow of the things to come, whereas the substance is of the Messiah. Do not let yourselves be condemned by any one set on self-abasement and worship of angels, [beings] he saw [when] going in [to the heavens], someone puffed up to no purpose by carnal imaginations, and not holding to the head from which all the body, nourished and knit together throughout its joints and ligaments, grows the growth of God. If, dying with Messiah, you left behind the elemental spirits of the world, why do you live as if still in the world? . . . If you have been raised [from the dead] with the Messiah, seek the things above, where the Messiah is, sitting to the right of God. Fix your mind on the things above, not those on earth. For you have died, and your life has been hidden with the Messiah in God. When the Messiah, our life, will be revealed then you too will be revealed with him in glory.

These passages show at a glance the immense difference between the baptism of the Baptist and that of Paul. The Baptist's rite was like the Old Testament immersions, except that it was specially instituted by God through a new prophet, and it removed sin, whereas they had removed impurity. Paul's baptism, by contrast, is a way of uniting with Jesus the Messiah, whom Paul conceives as "the spirit" (II Cor. 3.17; I Cor. 15.45). So Paul conceives union with the Messiah as possession by a spirit. The spirit lives inside the baptized and acts through them (most conspicuously, it speaks through them, making incomprehensible noises—a common symptom of schizophrenia). Thus the body of each possessed Christian is in effect a part (a "member," that is, a hand or foot or whatever) of the body of the Messiah, who lives and acts in them all.[1]

This basic concept Paul develops in different ways to meet different needs. In *Romans 6* he is protesting against a libertine interpretation of his teachings; he argues that union with the

1. Rom. 8.9,11,26; I Cor. 2.13; 3.16; 6.19; 12 entire; cf. Mk. 1.24f; 5.7f; 13.11.

Messiah involves participation in his death and resurrection; since "he died to sin," the new life must be one from which sin is excluded. In *I Corinthians 12* Paul is protesting against the arrogance of those who claimed to have special spiritual gifts; he argues that by union with the Messiah all Christians are made parts of the same body and therefore mutually dependent. In *Galatians 3* he is attacking opponents who prided themselves on keeping the Jewish law, so he argues that union with the Messiah sets all Christians free from the law and makes them all one and equal. Finally, in *Colossians 2–3* he is protesting against the introduction of some cult of the cosmic powers that conceived them as supernatural beings to be honored or placated by observance of the law. Therefore he argues that union with the Messiah involves participation in his nature, his death, and his resurrection. By nature he was superior to the cosmic powers, by death he stripped them off and subjected them, by resurrection he ascended above them and was hidden in God, where the Christians are hidden with him until the End. Consequently they should not subject themselves to inferior beings.

Some of these Pauline developments are obviously secondary. The notion that union with Jesus involves participation in his death and resurrection must have arisen after those events.[2] The deduction of mutual dependence from the analogy of a body looks like moralizing reflection to meet the needs of a developing community. The argument to prove Jewish and gentile Christians equal cannot have arisen until gentile conversion and Jewish snobbery created problems.[3] All these practical applications, different

2. There were some early Jewish Christians who never attributed any importance to Jesus' death, least of all as a sacrifice. They taught that he had come to abolish sacrifices and to institute a new means of salvation—by baptism. Such teaching looks like an extreme development of the Baptist's message (if baptism did remove sins it would make many sacrifices unnecessary), so it is not impossible that this may have been part of the secret teaching of Jesus.

3. Similarly I Cor. 10.1–4, omitted above because it does not speak directly of Christian baptism, shows the fundamental notion of union with the Messiah,

in each different passage, are possibly due to Paul. Certainly they do not come from Jesus himself.

By contrast to these, there is one basic notion common to all the passages: In baptism the initiate is possessed by the spirit of Jesus. This reflects beliefs about possession like those underlying the exorcism stories in Mark. Like them, it may have its background in Palestine and in Jesus' own teaching and practice. And there are five reasons for thinking it does.

1. Paul's baptism was first of all a ritual for union with Jesus; Jesus himself introduced another ritual for this same purpose.

2. The union in Paul's baptism was affected by the spirit, and the spirit was the cause and characteristic of Jesus' ministry.

3. The closest parallels to Paul's baptism are found in magical material, and there is considerable evidence that Jesus practiced magic.

4. Paul's baptism was connected with ascent into the heavens; Jesus was believed to have ascended, perhaps already in his lifetime.

5. Finally, Paul's baptism freed the recipient from the law, from which Jesus' disciples had been freed.

Let us look at these points more closely:

1. *Union with Jesus:* This was the essential thing in Paul's baptism. Where, then, did it come from? Did Paul either himself invent, or borrow from the pagan world this basic notion which is the fundamental and common element in all his references to baptism? Not likely. We should suppose that *this* was what he learned from Jesus' disciples when he was baptized. But if so, where did they get it (within three or four years of Jesus' death)? Certainly not from Judaism. No rite for union with any person is known to the Old Testament or to Palestinian Judaism, with one

developed by a type of theological theory that can hardly have been part of Jesus' teaching.

exception: the communion meal introduced by Jesus. Both baptism and communion have their closest parallels in magical material the like of which was unquestionably familiar in Palestine at Jesus' time; the Jews were famous as magicians and proud of it.

Spells in which a magician identifies himself with a spirit are plentiful in the magical papyri. A good example comes from *The Sacred Hidden Book of Moses called Eighth or Holy:*

And Thou, lord of life, ruler of the heavens and the earth and all those dwelling in them, whose righteousness is not turned aside, whose glorious name the Muses hymn, whom the eight guards escort, *e, o, ho, houh, Noun, Nauni, Amoun, Amauni,*[4] who hast the unerring truth, thy name and thy spirit rest upon the good. Enter my mind and my thoughts for the whole time of my life and perform for me all the desires of my soul, for Thou art I and I am Thou.

This does not look much like Jewish orthodoxy, but Jesus' communion meal ("the eucharist") looks even less. Commands like "Eat my body" and "Drink my blood" are obviously incompatible with the Old Testament and with rabbinic tradition. Their closest parallels again come from the magical papyri. For instance, take the following passage, from the London-and-Leiden magical papyrus, which exemplifies a type: One mingles various ingredients in a cup of wine and says over it an invocation.

I am he [the god of the temple] of Abydos . . . as to which the blood of [the god] Osiris bore witness . . . when it was poured into this cup, this wine. Give it, blood of Osiris [that] he gave to [the goddess] Isis to make her feel love in her heart for him . . . give it, the blood of so-and-so [here the magician put in his own name] to so-

4. Such jabberwocky is called "magical words." These cries (often, as here, including the names of outlandish deities) were used by magicians to work themselves into a state in which they believed they possessed the powers they claimed and enjoyed the experiences they desired. When their experiences resulted in disintegration of the personality they continued to utter similar sounds, involuntarily. Inarticulate utterances play similar roles in many primitive and enthusiastic groups, for instance, the Yippies.

and-so [the name of the recipient] in this cup, this bowl of wine, today, to make her feel love for him in her heart, the love that Isis felt for Osiris.

The essential identity of this with the communion miracle is obvious: the drink in the chalice, identified with the blood of the magician-deity, is given to the communicant so that the two may be united in love. No other known ancient texts come so close to the communion formula as do the magical conjurations of this sort.

Thus early Christianity has two rites for uniting the believer with Jesus. Both derive from magical practice, both show a similar break with traditional Judaism, and both must have been introduced within half a dozen years. Of these two rites, communion was certainly introduced by Jesus, so baptism, too, most likely came from him, as the Church claimed it did. This likelihood is increased by a number of sayings in which he speaks of his followers as identified with himself: "He that hears you, hears me," etc.

2. *The work of the spirit:* Paul's baptism "gave the spirit"; those who received it were thenceforth to be possessed, inhabited, and guided by a power not themselves, which expressed itself not only by inarticulate cries, but by radical alteration of their personalities. This notion is fundamental for Paul's thought. He comes back to it again and again, as the basic fact of Christian life. Where, then, did he get this strange idea? Old Testament immersions have nothing to do with the spirit, neither does Jewish proselyte baptism. In Qumran, the *Manual of Discipline* required cleansing by the spirit as a preparation for immersion to remove impurity, so the spirit must have come before the immersion. The Baptist's baptism did not give the spirit, either; it is contrasted with Christian baptism on this ground (Mk. 1.8; Acts 19.2ff; etc.). So when did the spirit come into connection with baptism?

It first appears immediately after the baptism of Jesus.[5] Jn. 1.33 makes the Baptist say explicitly that Jesus, on whom the spirit came down, is the one who will baptize others so that they too receive it. From his baptism on, Jesus is the man with the spirit. The spirit *drove* him into the wilderness to talk with other spirits. He made his reputation by casting out spirits, and he claimed to do so by the power of the holy spirit. He gave his disciples power over spirits and assured them that the spirit would speak through them (as the spirits of the demoniacs spoke through the demoniacs). This Markan material is further developed by the other synoptics and is supported by independent traditions in John.[6]

Jesus, therefore, was probably the one who made of baptism a rite in which the initiate became possessed by a spirit. By Paul's time the spirit was thought to be Jesus' spirit. Jesus probably had thought so, too. The stories of his baptism suggest, however, that he thought the spirit was "his" because it had come to him and possessed him, not because it was native to him. Outside reports speak of him sometimes as possessed, sometimes as "having" a demon; this same variation is common in accounts of shamans— some say the man has the demon, others, the demon has the man. The Gospel of Peter understood the end of Jesus' public career in accordance with its beginning: it translated his cry from the cross with the words, "My power, my power, you have left me!" ("Power" here means a supernatural being, a mighty spirit.)

3. *Magic:* Paul's baptism was unquestionably a rite that produced possession by a spirit. There are many such rites known from antiquity. Most of them come from the magical papyri; such possession was the goal of a major type of magic. Paul's baptism was therefore, by ancient standards, a magical rite. We know that Jesus introduced another magical rite—communion—and it seems likely

5. So in Mk. 1.10 and parallels, the Ebionite Gospel, and the Gospel according to the Hebrews.

6. Mk. 1.10ff; 3.22ff; 6.7; 1.23ff; 5.6ff; 13.11; Mt. 10.25; Lk. 10.17ff; Jn. 8.48; 10.20f; etc.

that he also introduced this magical baptism. The likelihood is increased by much other evidence that he practiced magic.

His practice has not been recognized because the Gospels do not say that he was a magician, nor do they represent him as using long spells or elaborate magical operations. But the Gospels were written by his followers who believed he was what many magicians claimed to be:—a god disguised as a man. Of course they did not represent him as a magician; magic was a criminal offense. As for spells and the like, many magicians did not use them either. Many magical texts are directions for securing the services of a spirit. Once the magician "has" his spirit he does not need spells; he can simply give orders, not only to his own spirit, but to the inferior ones whom it controls. And this is what Jesus was believed to do.[7]

Besides the reports that Jesus ordered spirits about, the miracle stories in the Gospels show many minor traits of magical procedures. A number of these have been pointed out by previous scholars: Jesus' curing by touch, manipulation, looking upward, sighing or groaning, use of Aramaic phrases in Greek, use of typically magical words, use of spittle in a salve, conspicuous use of the hands, touching the tongue, claiming to use "the finger of God," anger at the demons, prohibition of their return, requirement that the patients have "faith" (meaning "trust"), secrecy in performing the cures, performance in private and commands that the cures be kept secret, instructions to the disciples to pray and fast before exorcisms, the requirement of three-day or seven-day preparatory periods, the use of a sheet over the naked body as a costume for initiations, requiring the demons to tell their names, and so on and on.

But all these minor traits, in spite of their number, are not the decisive evidence. What really proves Jesus practiced magic is the essential content of most of the major stories in the Gospels. In Mark Jesus appears as one possessed by a spirit and thereby made

7. Mt. 8.8f; Lk. 7.7ff; Mk. 1.25,34; 3.12,22; 4.39; etc.

the son of a god; so do magicians in the magical papyri. Other stories say he was fathered by a god; the same was said of other magicians. Like them, he was driven by the spirit into the wilderness and there met and repulsed evil spirits; this is a typical pattern of shamanic initiation. And like the shamans he is sometimes represented as possessing a spirit, sometimes as himself possessed. Like other ancient magicians he lived as a wandering preacher with a circle of disciples, but was distinguished from ordinary preachers by his miraculous powers. Most of the various stories told of him are told of other magicians, and directions for their performance are given in the magical papyri. Among these are:

the power to make anyone he wanted follow him,
exorcism, even exorcism at a distance,
remote control of spirits and the power to order them about,
giving his disciples power over demons,
miraculous cures of hysterical conditions including fever, paralysis,
   hemorrhage, deafness, blindness, loss of speech,
raising the dead,
stilling storms,
walking on water,
miraculous provision of food,
miraculous escapes (his body could not be seized),
making himself invisible,
possessing the keys of the kingdom or of the heavens,
foreknowledge of his own fate, of disasters coming on cities, etc.,
knowledge of others' thoughts,
introduction of religious reforms and of new magical rites,
claiming to be united with others, so that he is in them and they in him,
claiming to be a god, or son of god, or united with a god, notably in
   statements beginning, "I am,"
claiming to be the only one who knows his god, or is known by his god,
claiming to be the image of the invisible god.

All these claims and stories and rites are those of a magician, not of a rabbi or a Messiah. Who ever heard of the Messiah's being an exorcist, let alone being eaten? The closest parallels in the Old Testament are to be found in the stories of the prophets, but here too the exorcistic and sacramental sides are completely lacking. There is no need to deny that Jesus first thought himself a prophet and later the Messiah, nor that he gave legal rulings; he probably did all three. But neither his imitations of the prophets nor his legal opinions nor his messianic belief nor all three together account for most, and the most important, of the stories about him, which are stories of a man who did the things magicians claimed to do.

His disciples went on telling such stories of his activities after his death. Many of them, especially in the gnostic wing of Christianity, went on practicing magic and revered Jesus as the great magician. Even in the comparatively "orthodox" catacombs he was customarily represented with a magician's rod. Jewish and pagan opinion unanimously believed him a magician. And even "orthodox" Christianity perpetuated many magical practices, not only exorcism, prophecy, miraculous cures, and the central rites of baptism and communion, but, for instance, Paul's handing his opponents over to Satan (I Cor. 5.3ff; cf. I Tim. 1.20), the practice of baptism on behalf of the dead (I Cor. 15.29), and that of "speaking with tongues," that is, of incomprehensible utterance "by the spirit" through the possessed believers. Paul thought this the supreme prayer of the Church (Rom. 8.26f.); we are given examples of it in the gnostic work, Pistis Sophia, and there the words of the spirit turn out to be well-known magical formulae. No doubt such magical practices did much to account for the persecutions of Christians throughout the Roman Empire.

To summarize: pagan and Jewish traditions alike represent Jesus as a magician, while Christian tradition represents him as what a successful magician would have claimed to be—the possessor of the holy spirit and himself a supernatural being, the son of a god. These reports are confirmed by the many minor magical traits of the miracle stories and, more importantly, by the whole outline of Jesus' career and the essential content of most of the stories about him, which are stories of things magicians claimed to do. Further confirmation comes from the history of Jesus' followers, who repeated and improved the legend of his magical prowess, continued themselves to practice magic, and were punished for it by the Roman authorities. Of Jesus' many magical actions the most important was the introduction of the eucharist, a rite of a well-known magical type, by which he thought to unite his followers to himself. Now baptism is another magical rite, intended to unite Jesus' followers to him by making his spirit possess them. It seems to have been practiced in Christianity at the latest within two or three years of Jesus' death, and there is no strong reason to doubt (and there are some reasons to believe) that it came in already during his lifetime. If we look for the person most likely to have introduced such a magical rite for such a purpose, the search will certainly lead us to Jesus himself.

4. *Ascent into the heavens:* Baptism not only gave Jesus' followers his spirit, but also got them into the kingdom in a special way—a way that made them greater even than the Baptist.

The kingdom of God *par excellence* was the heavens, where God himself was, and his throne and paradise and the angels and the souls of the blessed, where his will was done and his peace maintained. From ancient times there had circulated through the near east and Greece stories of men who had ascended into the heavens and thereby secured secret knowledge and supernatural powers and had even become supernatural beings—angels or gods. Stories about such ascents had been common in the pious literature of Palestine for at least a century before Jesus' time.

They seem to have led to some sort of hypnotic technique by which men could give both themselves and others the illusion of having experienced such an ascent. Traces of this technique appear in Palestinian literature of the first centuries B.C., including that found at Qumran; Josephus probably refers to the Essenes' practice of it; there are a number of later Jewish handbooks for the journey, the *hekalot* books. There are also handbooks for the same purpose in the pagan magical papyri, and these so much resemble the Jewish handbooks that both seem to have come from a common source which cannot have been later than the first century B.C. So there was available in Jesus' time a pietistic magical technique for entering the kingdom of God *par excellence,* the heavens, and those who entered might expect to become supernaturally gifted. They could also take disciples with them and confer the same gifts on them; both the Jewish and the pagan handbooks give directions for this. But the angels were jealous of men and guarded the gates of the heavens. The magician had to overcome them on his way up, either by appropriate spells or by the power of his own spirit.

If Jesus used this technique to enable his followers to enter the kingdom, we should have an explanation of the hitherto inexplicable saying in Mt. 11.12, "From the days of John the Baptist until now the kingdom of the heavens can be forced and violent men can seize it." This is closely connected with the statement that no man born of woman is greater than the Baptist, but the least in the kingdom—the least "born of water *and the spirit*" (that is, of Jesus' baptism, as opposed to the Baptist's)—is greater than he.[8]

That Jesus did use this technique of ascent into the heavens is suggested by much indirect evidence. Such an ascent is the goal anticipated by much early Christian teaching. Jesus has ascended into the heavens; his followers hope to ascend—even, somehow, in this life. Jesus went as their leader and showed them the way.

8. Mt. 11.11; Lk. 7.28; Jn. 3.5f. The version in Lk. 16.16, "everyone pushes into it," is a reinterpretation from a later period when the kingdom has been identified with the successful Church.

Some of them actually claimed to have ascended and based on this their other claims for authority.[9]

The claim to have ascended into the heavens was often made by magicians, especially shamans, and therefore fits Jesus' character and career. We should, in fact, be surprised had he not made it. The practice would explain both the secret character of Jesus' baptism and the way it worked. It would also explain why both Paul and his opponents should have had the odd notion that their ascents into the heavens somehow proved they were apostles of Jesus. It would also explain Paul's interpretation of baptism as an ascent into the heavens (Col. 2.9–3.4), an interpretation which may go back to Paul's own baptism about A.D. 35.

The stories of Jesus' transfiguration seem distorted reflections of such an illusory ascent into the heavens, together with a few disciples. And there are three passages—Phil. 2.5–11; I Tim. 3.16; Jn. 3.13—which imply that Jesus had already ascended into the heavens in his lifetime (see also Jn. 6.38,42,58,62, and 10.36). These passages can be shown to reflect a connection of Jesus with Enoch, the most famous of Palestinian travelers through the heavens. This primitive connection has been overlaid in Paul and John by later theories about a preexistent Messiah, but in these verses the authors momentarily neglect their theories and reflect the earlier Palestinian tradition of a man taken up to the heavens, transformed into a supernatural being, and sent back to earth for the salvation of men, voluntarily submitting himself to this humiliation, and therefore once again exalted. This may well have been an early interpretation of Jesus' experience of ascent; indeed, it may have been that of Jesus himself. His practice of magic would have been perfectly compatible with the popular piety of his time and he would of course have tried to understand himself in the terms of the figures that piety presented: the prophet was

9. Heb. 2.10; 12.22f; II Pet. 1.11; Jn. 14.1–5; II Cor. 12.1–5; Col. 2.18; Apoc. 4.1ff.

one such figure, the Messiah was another, Enoch was a third; they could easily be combined, and his peculiar psychological experiences doubtless led him to combine them.

Finally, it seems that Jesus took some of his disciples with him—that is, he suggested to them illusions like those he himself experienced, so that they saw him, as in the transfiguration story, above the clouds, blazing with glory and talking with Moses and Elijah. This explains their later visions of him risen from the dead and ascending into the heavens. The similarity of these later visions to the transfiguration story has often been noticed and the later visions require explanation. They were not the sort of thing that could be expected from the followers of any pious rabbi. When Rabbi Akiba, perhaps the most revered figure in the whole rabbinic tradition, was executed by the Romans a century after Jesus' time, none of his disciples saw him risen from the dead or ascending into the heavens. That Jesus' disciples did see him so was probably due to their special preparation—their baptismal visions, now reflected in the transfiguration stories. Consequently Paul's notion of baptism as an ascent into the heavens will have been derived ultimately from Jesus.

5. *Liberation from the law:* Paul's baptism freed those baptized from any obligation to obey the Mosaic law. Paul explained this by the theory that they shared in Jesus' death—the explanation therefore must be later than the death. But the primary notion is not likely to have been Paul's invention; it runs counter to his Pharisaic upbringing and his moralizing temperament. Therefore we may suppose it was part of the teaching about baptism that he had received. Jesus' freedom from the law probably began with his ascent into the heavens (entrance of the kingdom) conceived as a passage from this world or age, subject to the law, to the coming world or age of liberty. A century later Rabbi Elisha ben Abuyah entered paradise and consequently threw over the law and became a libertine. (Like Jesus, even after this he continued to be

consulted on legal problems.) So the liberty of Jesus' disciples will have resulted from their identification with him in his baptism and their participation in his entrance of the kingdom.

Many stories and sayings in the Gospels represent Jesus as free of the law and as declaring or defending the freedom of his disciples. "The law and the prophets were [only] until John [the Baptist], from then on the kingdom of God is proclaimed," and is available to those who will use violence. The new message is the new wine, not to be put into the old skin of Judaism; it is the new garment not to be mutilated to patch up the old. Therefore the Son of Man (Jesus) is lord of the sabbath, can forgive sins, and does not come, like the Baptist, in "the way of righteousness," but "eating and drinking." He is a friend of publicans (Jews who cooperated with the Roman government) and sinners. His yoke, by contrast to that of the law, is light. The law came by Moses, but grace by Jesus. He alone has revealed the hitherto unknown Father. His followers shall know the truth and the truth will make them free of the law.[10]

Such sayings are balanced, though, by many others which imply that the Mosaic law is still in force. Some of the legalistic ones are secondary; they come from a rapprochement between the Jerusalem church and the Pharisees, in and after the forties A.D. But some must be original. Yet the sayings on the presence of the kingdom and its consequences must also be original; they are the most peculiar and characteristic element in Jesus' teaching. Consequently we have to explain the coexistence of these two bodies of material.[11] The most likely explanation is that the legalistic material represents Jesus' teaching for "those outside." For them he held that the law

10. Lk. 16.16; Mt. 11.12f; Mk. 2.22; Lk. 5.36; Mk. 2.28; 2.1ff; Mt. 11.18f; Mk. 2.15f; Mt. 11.29f; Jn. 1.17f; Lk. 10.22; Jn. 8.31f.
11. This question is discussed more fully in my article, "Jesus' Attitude Towards the Law," in the Papers of the Fourth World Congress of Jewish Studies, Jerusalem, 1967, vol. I, pp. 241–244.

was still binding and he interpreted it as did the other legal teachers of his time; about one point he would have a more lenient opinion, about another, a stricter one—such variation appears in the rulings of almost all ancient rabbis. But he himself was free of the law, and so were those who had been baptized with his spirit. The contradictions of the present Gospels probably result from a gradual seepage of secret material into texts originally meant for outsiders. This is indicated by the fact that the material for insiders is more prominent in the later elements of the Gospels than in the earlier. Another example of such seepage might be seen in the addition to Mark of the secret text, if that was an addition. But in spite of such occasional leaks, our best evidence for the secret teaching of Jesus is not the Gospels, but the letters of Paul (a whole generation earlier than the Gospels), and it was probably from Jesus' secret teaching and practice that Paul derived, through the intermediation of Jesus' immediate followers, his notion that baptism freed the baptized from the requirements of the law.

Thus from the differences between Paul's baptism and that of the Baptist, and from the scattered indications in the canonical Gospels and the secret Gospel of Mark, we can put together a picture of Jesus' baptism, "the mystery of the kingdom of God." It was a water baptism administered by Jesus to chosen disciples, singly and by night. The costume, for the disciple, was a linen cloth worn over the naked body. This cloth was probably removed for the baptism proper, the immersion in water, which was now reduced to a preparatory purification. After that, by unknown ceremonies,[12] the disciple was possessed by Jesus' spirit and so united with Jesus. One with him, he participated by hallucination

---

12. To judge from the *hekalot* and Qumran texts, the magical papyri and the Byzantine liturgy, these will have been mainly the recitation of repetitive, hypnotic prayers and hymns. The magical tradition also prescribes, in some instances, interference with breathing. Manipulation, too, was probably involved; the stories of Jesus' miracles give a very large place to the use of his hands.

in Jesus' ascent into the heavens, he entered the kingdom of God, and was thereby set free from the laws ordained for and in the lower world. Freedom from the law may have resulted in completion of the spiritual union by physical union. This certainly occurred in many forms of gnostic Christianity; how early it began there is no telling.

13

The Secret Tradition: Conclusion

Once I had got at the secret of Jesus' magical practice it was easy to understand why there was a secret tradition in early Christianity. Almost from the beginning of Jesus' ministry there must have been an inner circle (Jesus' closest followers to whom he had given the mystery), one or more outer circles (less intimate followers, family, and well-disposed acquaintances to whom the secret was not revealed), and finally "those outside" (the indifferent or hostile people of the surrounding world).

This new understanding of the early Christian group and its private practices explained a great deal that had been puzzling in early Christianity, but it also raised new problems. For instance: Jesus' baptism had been a secret, individual initiation that admitted the recipient immediately to the kingdom of the heavens; baptism in the early churches was given to entire households at once and merely admitted them to the Church. How can this change be explained? Again, Jesus was the man of the spirit, but the spirit was a power peculiar to him, whereas in the early churches it was a phenomenon of the behavior of whole congregations. How can this change be explained? And why do Acts and John insist that the spirit was not given until after Jesus' death, resurrection, and ascension?[1]

1. Acts 1.4f; 2 entire; 11.16; Jn. 7.39; 14.16f,26; 15.26; 16.7,13; 20.22.

Some of the answers we shall never know. From the history of Christianity between Jesus' death and the letters of Paul we have only the contradictory resurrection stories in the Gospels and the handful of traditions selected and remodeled by the author of Acts. Conclusive proof of what really happened is therefore impossible. But a theory that explains the sprinkling of preserved data has at least a chance of being correct.

The first of the data that have to be explained are the resurrection visions. They are best understandable as consequences of Jesus' baptismal practice, reflections of the visions he suggested to the young men he initiated.

After the resurrection stories comes the ascension story in Acts 1. This is another piece of the same cloth.

With Acts 2 we reach the story of the coming of the spirit as a group phenomenon. This looks like a late reflection of reports about the "speaking with tongues" in Paul's churches—reports the author did not correctly understand, since he turned the incomprehensible sounds uttered by the possessed into a super-language thought by all its hearers to be their native tongue. So what really has to be explained is not the imagined miracle of Acts 2, but the appearance of hysterical symptoms as group phenomena in the early churches. Critical scholarship generally has been quite unable to explain this "coming of the spirit"; it has merely identified the type of behavior and recorded that (for reasons unknown) it "came."

The reasons now can be guessed, especially if Acts is right in reporting that these phenomena began with the first group in Jerusalem. That was a congregation of which many members had been prepared for group possession by their experience of individual possession in Jesus' baptism. Jesus seems to have had a peculiar attraction for and power over schizophrenics. Hence his "exorcisms" (his ability to quiet persons whose suppressed impulses had broken through their rational control and expressed themselves in violent and destructive actions explained as the work of "demons"). Hence, too, his following of "women who had been cured of evil spirits" (Lk. 8.2).

The stories of his disciples' sudden, total abandonment of their ordinary lives to follow him (Mk. 1.16ff.; 2.14; Jn. 1.43) probably reflect the same power and indicate an instability in the disciples' characters that explains why they yielded to possession by Jesus in baptisms. Their baptismal experiences will in turn explain the possession of whole groups of them by his spirit after his death. Such group hysteria usually begins with individuals in the group; their visions and other symptoms are contagious—cf. the history of the witchcraft trials. Mass conversions followed. Both converts and the original followers, when they went abroad, communicated the psychological infection to the circles they formed in other provinces. Paul presumably caught it in Jerusalem: his first serious attack occurred while on the way to Damascus; he later spread the symptoms through Asia Minor and Greece.

This explains why the spirit is identified with Jesus, as it is by Paul (I Cor. 6.17; 15.45; II Cor. 3.17f). Jesus had originally been the source of these experiences. When the sudden, discontinuous changes of personality, originally connected with him, recurred as a group phenomenon in the circle of those who had depended on him for such excitement, he was of course supposed to be the cause. But this was a historical inference. As time went on and personal memories of Jesus faded, the spirit became an independent personality like the "demons" of the demoniacs; it pushed Jesus aside. This can be seen happening already in Paul. For, unlike Jesus, the spirit was alive and present. It spoke to the churches, did miracles, was the source of wisdom, and guide of private life.[2] So as the churches grew, the importance of the present, active spirit

2. Apoc. 2.7ff; I Cor. 12.8ff; Gal. 5.18ff; etc.

grew with them, while its connection with Jesus receded into the background—a memory for the very few he had initiated, a dogma for the many new converts.

Accordingly for Acts the spirit—meaning the supposed cause of the group phenomena—is something given after Jesus' death, for only then did the *group* attacks begin. (The author of Luke and Acts said nothing about Jesus' baptisms; they were part of the secret teaching. He also concealed what he knew about Paul's theology.)[3] In John, by contrast, the author's insistence that the spirit was not given until after Jesus' death and ascension is probably the result of polemic. That is why it is so emphatic: 7.39; 14.16f,26; 15.26; 16.7,13; 20.22. The author was at loggerheads with some of Jesus' original disciples, among them Thomas, or Thomas' followers. He was not himself an immediate disciple; he had to appeal to an unnamed disciple as his authority (21.24) and to make Jesus declare that those who had believed without seeing were more blessed than those like Thomas who had seen (20.29). Therefore he also appealed to the spirit, which he could claim for himself, against the original disciples' reports about Jesus. Jesus, he maintained, always spoke in parables, but the spirit was to lead the disciples to the whole truth (16.12f, 25). And therefore it was most important for this author that the spirit should have been given only after Jesus' death.

Once the group phenomena got under way, they radically changed the character of the sect. Psychological contagion reportedly made converts of thousands at once (Acts 2.41; 4.4). The outer circles of the Christian complex were vastly enlarged, whereas the innermost circle, those who had received the secret baptism, been admitted to the kingdom and freed from the law, must have grown very slowly.

3. On this see my article, "The Reasons for the Persecution of Paul," in *Studies in Mysticism and Religion Presented to G. Scholem*, Jerusalem, 1967, pp. 261–268.

No doubt some of Jesus' initiates had learned the technique of ascent and hypnotic suggestion from him and were able to carry on his practice. But his practice took time. A whole night was needed for each initiate. So the secret baptisms of a few individuals, one by one, were soon overshadowed by the mass conversions in the meetings of the churches. The converts had to be taken into the sect. Since they had not yet *ritually* entered the kingdom, many would think them, by Jesus' standards, still subject to the law. On the other hand, they had been possessed by Jesus; he lived in them, they were parts of his body, they were "in" him, so they must be in the kingdom and free from the law. Here was the basis for a deep and long-lasting dispute as to the liability of ordinary Christians to observe the law. Since Jesus had not foreseen group possession by his spirit, no pronouncements of his on the subject were available. But there was his example. He himself had gone to the Baptist for purification, and had used the Baptist's rite as the first part of his own. Since the Baptist had used it for great crowds it must have been relatively short and simple. So a reference to Jesus was added to the baptismal formula and with this change it was given at once to all the new converts, while the long, secret rite was reserved (as it had been from the beginning) for a chosen few.

The consequent situation appears in Acts 10, the story of the conversion of the family and friends of the pagan Cornelius. In the midst of Peter's sermon to them, the spirit suddenly seized them. What was left for Peter to do? Baptism was anticlimactic, it was merely "the water," but it still had to be used as a purification. For "who could deny the water" to those who had already received the spirit? (Acts 10.44–48; 11.15–18.)

Not all converts were so fortunate. Any ecstatic cult is likely to attract a lot of would-be ecstatics who never make the grade. Further, as Christianity grew, more and more people came into it because of family connections or friends or various practical reasons that had little to do with the spirit. The only thing that happened to such converts when they entered was the short baptismal ritual. As they increased in numbers, baptism became the decisive fact in admission to the community and therefore to the life of the Church. This entailed—tacitly, of course—a new interpretation of the old terms. The kingdom in the heavens was replaced by the kingdom present in this world; the spirit of Jesus as an experienced supernatural power was replaced by the spirit, as an entity separate from Jesus, not directly experienced, but supposed to be present in the Church; entrance of the Church replaced entrance of the kingdom; to join the Church was to become a member of a body inhabited *ex officio* by the spirit, so no special signs of its presence in the convert were required.

The further stages of this development are well known. As Christianity settled down to the continuation of life in this world, the excitement rapidly diminished and the spirit, as a group phenomenon, became rare. By A.D. 90 or thereabouts Luke no longer understood the Pauline tradition about "speaking with tongues." Individual prophets continued to flourish well into the second century, but they ran into more and more trouble with the growing church organizations and by the beginning of the third century they were likely to be excommunicated. The administration —as usual—won, and the spirit first became a legal fiction and later was relegated to the Trinity.

Even the beginnings of this development must have been unpleasant for Jesus' immediate followers who had been the original leaders of the Jerusalem group, had received the mystery and entered the kingdom and seen the visions and been the centers from which the spirit spread. When the spirit went public, their control of the company became less secure, when it began to be taken for granted as a consequence of an administrative procedure, they came in danger of displacement. For a time they were saved by the belief that they had supernatural powers. Not only were they famous for miraculous cures, but Peter was even rumored to have struck two people dead—that put the fear of God into the rest of the church (Acts 5.11). But these very powers increased the growth of the outer circle with its exoteric attitude.

A particularly sensitive point must have been the question of obedience to the law. There is no telling just how Jesus (and those of his circle who were in the kingdom and exempt from the law) got on with the outer circles of followers for whom the law was still binding. The texts of the Gospels were probably secretive about this to begin with and are now so much contaminated by esoteric material that no clear determination of the original divisions is possible. For the existence of a libertine circle at the center of a legalist group there are numerous examples, both in Judaism and elsewhere; the relationship may be maintained by anything from ordinary hypocrisy to outré theological theory. For Jesus' followers, the one thing reasonably sure is that the libertinism of the inner circle got them into trouble with the law. This explains another neglected problem in early Christianity: the Jewish persecution.

Why should the early Christians have been persecuted not only by the Jewish authorities, but by private pietists like Paul? There seems no likelihood that Christianity ever posed a serious threat of political revolution—certainly it did not do so after Jesus' death. The persecution by Jews, not only in Jerusalem, but also throughout the Roman empire, has to be explained on religious grounds. But holding odd beliefs about the Messiah is no offense against Jewish law. And the reasons for persecutions given by Acts are mostly inadequate. This raises the suspicion that something is being concealed. We may suspect that what was concealed was the teaching that the kingdom had already come and the law had been abolished for those in Jesus.[4]

If this was the teaching of Jesus' immediate followers, we could

4. Mk. 2.10,19,28; II Thess. 2.2; Acts 21.21,28.

then explain why the attitude of the Pharisees toward the Jerusalem church shifted from bitter hostility and persecution about A.D. 35 to friendliness, if not cooperation, about A.D. 55. Between those dates fell the persecution by Herod Agrippa I (A.D. 41–44), for which Acts gives no explanation. This drove Peter, Jesus' disciple, out of the city, and leadership of the church was taken by James, Jesus' brother, who had not believed during Jesus' lifetime, but had come into the church after Jesus' death. He was famous for his devotion to the temple and his traditional Jewish piety. It is not inconceivable that the legalist party within the Jerusalem church may have asked their friends in other Jewish parties—particularly the Pharisees, who had much influence with Herod Agrippa I—for a little timely persecution to help get rid of their libertine rivals.

James' succession to control of the church probably marked the triumph in Jerusalem of the legalist party over the libertines and of the new converts over the original disciples of Jesus. This was followed by the appearance in the mission fields of representatives of James who at Antioch frightened even Peter and Barnabas into observing the Jewish food laws (Gal. 2.11–13), and who probably circulated through Asia Minor and Greece, teaching that converts to Christianity must observe at least some parts of the Mosaic law.

Thus Christianity was split into a number of parties. From Acts 21.15–26 and other evidence it is customary to distinguish the following: first the extreme legalists, whom James in Acts is trying to pacify; they maintained that the law was still binding on all Christians, therefore they must have denied either that the kingdom .could as yet be entered or that entrance of it put one beyond the law. Second, the party of James who maintained that the *appearance* of obeying the law was to be preserved. (Acts' account of James is not to be trusted; it is probably malicious, but it may not be wholly misleading; the concerns for appearance and for living at peace with one's neighbors are important in Jewish law.) Third, the position of Paul: there is no need to appear to obey the law unless apparent disobedience would lead you into danger or your fellow Christians into sin. But one may obey when obedience seems politic, provided one does so with a clear understanding that obedience and disobedience are of no importance for salvation. Peter and Barnabas are commonly supposed to have held some mediate position(s) between Paul and James; of whatever positions (if any) they did hold there is no reliable evidence.

On this customary list of parties, two observations must be made. First, James' reported position practically supposes that the doctrine about the liberty of those in the kingdom will be kept secret. The extreme legalist party in James' church was probably the source of sayings like Mt. 23.2: "The scribes and the Pharisees sit on Moses' seat; all things whatsoever they tell you, these do and observe." Such a party would hardly have lived at peace with another which held that obedience to the law was optional, unless the latter opinion was masked by obedience and kept secret. Similarly the position of Paul is congenial to secrecy and Paul seems to have kept some of his teachings and practices secret. Some members of his churches did not know that the eating of things sacrificed to idols was essentially harmless (I Cor. 8.7). Others were "babes" who were ignorant of the mysteries revealed by the spirit, of the things to be revealed at the end, and of their own freedom from the law (I Cor. 2.6–16; 3.1–4; 8.7; cf. 13.8–13). Evidently·there was a good deal of difference between what he preached when founding a community and what he explained later; his doctrine of Christian liberty must have been kept at first for an inner circle, and he sometimes, at least, attributed primary importance to the mass missionary work. He could even say, in a moment of passionate argument, that he was not sent to baptize, but to preach the Gospel (I Cor. 1.17). But in the same breath he admits that he did baptize (1.14ff), and he goes on to tell his converts that some of them, at least, are not fit to hear the wisdom of God that he speaks in the mystery, as opposed to his ordinary preaching (2.1–3.4). Was the mystery the full form of Jesus' baptism, as opposed to the short Christianized version of the Baptist's rite? We cannot tell.

A second observation on the list of early Christian parties is that it follows Acts and therefore neglects the libertine party or parties to the left of Paul—groups like that against which Paul defends himself in I Cor. 8ff. Acts' silence about such parties (except for an occasional veiled reference like 20.29ff) is not accidental. One of the author's purposes was to persuade his Roman readers that Christianity was morally admirable and politically innocent (18.-14f; 23.29; 25.25; 26.31). Therefore the libertinism, usually scandalous and occasionally criminal, was concealed. And no writings from the libertine side of primitive Christianity have survived —an understandable misfortune. Consequently scholars have denied the existence of the libertine side and have treated the references to it in the New Testament as references to particular abuses in practice or corruptions in doctrine peculiar to the single churches in connection with which they are mentioned.

Not every warning against moral turpitude implies the existence of a libertine sect—sin occurs even in legalistic communities. But the arguments of Jude and I Corinthians cannot be explained by individual offenses unconnected with theological theories. They prove the existence of theoretical libertinism. Since it existed, the other passages that may refer to it have to be examined. Here is a list of those in which polemic against it is fairly clear.

Mt. 5.19: "Whoever breaks one of the least of these commandments [of the law] and *teaches* men to break them shall be called the least in the kingdom of the heavens." Since the offender is in the kingdom, he must be a Christian teacher. This shows why the Christians had to expect abuse and resign themselves to being the objects of scandal

(5.11), and be warned against going bad (5.13). It also explains why Matthew added, to the blessing on those who hunger and thirst, the words "for righteousness," and to the commandment to seek the kingdom of God, the words "and his righteousness" (5.6; 6.33; contrast the parallels in Luke).

Mt. 7.15–27: "Beware of false prophets who come to you dressed up like sheep, but inside they are ravenous wolves. You can recognize them by the fruits they bear; does anybody get grapes from brambles? . . . Not everyone who says to me, 'Lord, Lord,' will enter the kingdom of the heavens, but [only] the one who does the will of my Father who is in the heavens. Many will say to me in that day, 'Lord, Lord, have we not prophesied in your name and cast out demons in your name and done many miracles in your name?' And then I shall confess to them, 'I never knew you. Depart from me, you who break the law.' " Evidently these teachers pretended to observe the law, and also claimed supernatural (magical) powers, but their secret teaching and practice was libertine.

Lk. 7.36–50: While Jesus was dining with a Pharisee, a woman who was a sinner came in and anointed Jesus' feet. The Pharisee thought, "If this man were a prophet he would have known that this woman does not keep the purity laws, and therefore would not have let her touch him, since her touch communicates her impurity." Jesus, knowing his thoughts, asked him, "A creditor had two debtors; one owed him fifty dollars, the other, five hundred. Since neither could repay, he cancelled both debts. Which, then, will love him more?" The Pharisee said, "I suppose, the one to whom he forgave more." Jesus answered, "You suppose correctly . . . So this woman's many sins are forgiven because she loved [me?] much, but a man to whom little is forgiven loves little." This story has been edited. At first it dealt with ritual impurity. It was made over to illustrate forgiveness of sins. Then the conclusion was changed. From the (false) premise, "The more a man is forgiven, the more he will love," the conclusion must have been, "Those who have most to be forgiven—the greatest sinners—can love most." Luke thought this a dangerous doctrine, so he replaced it by the innocuous *non sequitur* now in the text. However, he preserved a lot of material suggesting that the kingdom was primarily for sinners: *5.32*, Jesus "came not to call the righteous, but sinners *to repentance"; 15.4ff*, the lost sheep; *15.8ff*, the lost coin; *15.7,10*. "There is [more] joy in heaven over one sinner who repents [than over ninety-nine righteous]"; *15.12ff*, the prodigal son; *16.1ff*, the unjust steward. Here, too, Luke made editorial changes, as can be shown by comparisons with Matthew. He added *to repentance* in 5.32; he deleted *more* in 15.7, and deleted the whole second half of the sentence in 15.10. These changes show he was troubled by the libertine implications of these passages; presumably they were live issues in some churches he knew.

Acts 20.29f: Paul is made to tell the elders of the church of Ephesus, "I know that after my departure cruel wolves will come among you and will not spare the flock; and from you yourselves will come men teaching perverted things, to draw to themselves the disciples." This pseudo-prophecy is an attack on Christian teachers working in Ephesus when Acts was written. Cf. Mt. 7.15ff; II Thess. 2.1f; 3.6ff; II Tim. 2.16ff; etc.

Rom. 3.8: Paul is attacking people who say that he teaches, "Let us do evil that good may come." From the context it appears that this good is salvation by grace and free forgiveness of sins. If the teaching was not Paul's—he says it was not—whose was it? Did it come from the libertines? They might have got it from the principle that love results from forgiveness, so the greatest sinner, who has most to be forgiven, is capable of the greatest love (above, on Lk. 7.36ff). *In 6.1* Paul rejects another suggestion, "Let us remain in sin, so that more grace may be given [us]." This looks like another piece of the same teaching. In *8.1* we find an objection and answer, "But then, [isn't it true that,] 'There is no condemnation for those in Messiah Jesus?' [Yes, it is true,] because" etc. The objection looks as if it were a well-known principle, probably preached by the libertines, which Paul had to 'explain.' *In 8.12* the notion that we are not debtors to the flesh appears suddenly and without reference to what has preceded. Who said we were debtors to the flesh, that Paul should deny it? Some libertine gnostics said so in the second century, and their doctrine may have reflected first-century teaching; something similar was found by the Carpocratians in Mt. 5.25f. Since there are so many references to libertine teachings in the first half of Romans, some of the moral teachings of the second half may refer to them, too—notably the attacks on pride, on rejection of the civil law, on lasciviousness, and on other behavior likely to cause scandal. These can hardly refer to conditions in the Roman church, which Paul did not know.

I Cor. 5.2: Some of the Corinthians were proud that incest was being practiced in their church. In *5.11* Paul had to warn them against people in the church who were practicing fornication, idolatry, etc. Such people, he had to insist, would never get into the kingdom of God— apparently others thought they would, or had. *6.9f,* "Don't be fooled," shows there was an opposed teaching. *6.12f,* "All things are permissible," is probably one of its premises which Paul must "explain." *8.1ff* indicates another premise, that knowledge has freed the initiates from the law, cf. Jn. 8.32. *15:32ff* shows the conclusion the libertines drew from this, "Let us eat and drink, for tomorrow we die" (and need fear no condemnation). Paul declares that the Christians who teach such things have ignorance, not knowledge, of God; the declaration connects the teaching with 8.1ff. Cf. Mt. 11.19.

Gal. 5.13ff: "You were called to freedom, brothers—only not to the freedom that provides a pretext for the flesh." Paul was evidently aware of the danger of a libertine interpretation of his doctrine.

Phil. 3.18ff: "There are many going about [as Christian teachers] of whom I have often told you, and now tell you with tears, that they are enemies of the cross of Christ,[5] their destination is destruction, their god is their belly, and their glory is in their shame." Presumably liber-

5. See note 2, chap. 12, above.

tines. *3.12* may be an anticipation, in an argument against legalists, of the danger of a libertine interpretation.

II Thess. 3.6ff: "We exhort you, brothers, . . . to take a position against every brother who behaves improperly," especially those living off the community and refusing to work. See above, on Acts 20.29f.

Ephesians 5.1–20: A long attack on teachers who are trying to deceive the Ephesians (5.6) and lead them into sexual and other offenses— "It is shameful even to mention the things they do in secret." These are clearly libertines and the passage must refer to specific persons. Contrast the generalizing morality of Col. 3.5–17, which the author of Ephesians was reworking.

I Tim. 1.19f: This exhortation to keep *both* the faith *and* a clear conscience is presumably directed against the followers of Hymenaeus and Alexander, whom it taunts with their teachers' misfortunes, supposed to have been caused by Paul's magic—he handed them over to Satan. Hymenaeus appears again in II Tim. 2.17.

II Tim. 2.16–4.4: Hymenaeus and Philetus deny the resurrection, practice injustice, teach impiety, and give free rein to childish desires. They and others like them practice all the sins in spite of their Christian training (3.5). They are magicians like Iannes and Iambres, the legendary opponents of Moses (3.8), and their teaching that the resurrection has already taken place probably refers to a magical initiation in baptism. This links them to the men attacked in I Cor. 15; II Thess. 3.6ff; Acts 20.29; etc.

James 2.14ff; 3.13–18: The opponent, who thinks good works unnecessary provided one has faith, may be Paul, but there is so much evidence for libertinism that identification is impossible.

I Pet. 2.11–16: The warning that Christian liberty should not be made a cloak for wrongdoing shows that the author was aware of libertinism, though he did not think it an immediate danger to the group for which he was writing.

II Pet. 1.5–11: The insistence that one must have virtue as well as faith, and continence as well as gnosis, is probably aimed at some libertine teachers attacked in verse 9: they have neither virtue nor continence, are purblind, and have forgotten that they needed to be cleansed of their former sins (which, therefore, they should not renew).

II Pet. 2–3 and Jude: This anti-libertine tract was popular; two versions of it were canonized. It shows the range and bitterness of the polemic. The libertines are false prophets and give Christianity a bad reputation; they will receive punishments like those given the fallen angels and the cities of Sodom and Gomorrah, whose sins they imitate. They have no respect for the heavenly powers and they misunderstand Christian liberty, thinking it an opportunity for carnal indulgence. They follow the example of the sinners of the Old Testament, notably Balaam. They are empty clouds, wandering stars, for whom the blackness of great darkness is reserved forever.

I Jn. 1.6,8,10: The author is attacking opponents who claim to have communion with Jesus, but "walk in darkness," i.e., have practices he disapproves. Yet they claim to be sinless. This looks like perfectionist, libertine theology. They claim to have known Jesus, but do not keep his commandments; they come from Christian congregations, but are antichrists (*2.18f*), denying that Jesus was the Messiah (*2.22*). They sin deliberately (*3.7ff*) and are false prophets inspired by the spirit of the great Antichrist (*4.1ff*) and of this lower world. Cf. II Jn. 7.

Apoc. 2.6,14f,20ff: The Christian congregation at Thyatira, a little town of western Asia Minor, tolerates a lady whom the author calls Jezebel. She claims to be a prophetess and teaches her followers that whoring and idolatry are permissible. This has been going on for some time. Similar teachings, like those of the wicked Balaam (cf. Jude), are also striking root in Pergamum, a much bigger place where there are perhaps two sects of this sort. Similar teachers have been snubbed at Ephesus; the Nicholas mentioned here was early and perhaps correctly identified with the one in Acts 6.5.

Besides these passages there are many more which probably refer to libertines, but which I have excluded because the reference is not certain. These clear passages are enough to show that libertine Christianity was widespread and ancient. It is attested in Ephesus, Corinth, Thessalonica, Pergamum, and Thyatira. It must have been important in Syria, whence came Matthew and the source of II Peter and Jude. There is a likelihood that it was important in some areas from which the "orthodox" did not choose to preserve material—Egypt, for instance. It is attacked by Matthew, Luke, Acts, Paul (in five letters), Ephesians, I and II Timothy, James, I and II Peter, I and II John, Jude, and the Apocalypse.

To try to explain all this as a result of misunderstanding of Paul is hopeless. Paul complains that his name and his sayings are being misused by the libertines. He does not complain of misunderstanding, but of deliberate misrepresentation, and he does not write as if the persons concerned were his former disciples. But if the misrepresentation was deliberate it was presumably in the interest of some already existing position. And now we know from whom that position derived: a figure earlier and even more influential than Paul, and a figure notorious for his libertine teaching and practice. He broke the Sabbath, he neglected the purity rules, he refused to fast, made friends with publicans and sinners, and was known as "a gluttonous man and a winebibber." He not only taught his disciples that the law had come to an end with the Baptist, and that the least in the kingdom was greater than the Baptist, but he also administered a baptism of his own—"the mystery of the kingdom of God"—by which he enabled some of his disciples, united with himself, to enter the kingdom and to enjoy his own freedom from the law.

Therefore, in our picture of pre-Pauline Christianity, alongside the legalistic interpretation of the religion we must set the libertine. The legalistic interpretation went back to the (mainly Pharisaic?) converts of the Jerusalem church, and appealed to the tradition of Jesus' exoteric teaching. The libertine interpretation went back to Jesus himself and preserved and developed elements of his esoteric teaching. It was dominant in the Jerusalem church in the earliest days, but it lost its hold as the small group of Jesus' original, initiated disciples was outnumbered by the new converts under the leadership of Jesus' brother, James, and it went underground when Peter, the leader of the original disciples, was driven out of the city by the persecution under Herod Agrippa I. This libertine tradition, its strength, its diffusion, its unanimity, and its evident age, is explicable only by our understanding of Jesus' teaching about the mystery of the kingdom. This is strong evidence that the understanding is correct.

Another problem of early Christianity cleared up by the same understanding is the "loss" of all writings of Jesus and his immediate disciples. That this presents a problem has sometimes been recognized. The fact that Jesus and his followers founded a surviving sect makes the loss of *all* their writings surprising indeed. It is most unlikely that they were all illiterate; literacy was common even among the lower classes in the Roman world. So what became of their writings? Most likely they were suppressed. But why would Christians have suppressed them? Because of their libertine content. James, in Jerusalem, probably did much of the cleaning up.

James' works, too, were wiped out by the great Jewish revolts of 66–74 and 132–135 in Palestine and of 115–117 in Egypt, Cyrene, Cyprus, Syria, and Mesopotamia. These seem to have ruined most of the legalistic side of primitive Christianity. Asia Minor was the only area in the near east where a large Jewish population survived relatively undisturbed. But Asia Minor had been the scene of Paul's most successful work and Paul was the most dangerous opponent of the libertines. In the conflict between the libertine and the legalist interpretations, he represented the safe, sane, and socially acceptable compromise. He accepted the presence of the kingdom, but rejected those who made it an excuse for refusing to work. He also accepted the legalists' expectation of a kingdom to come in the future, but he dropped the nationalistic and political side of it, which was to involve the legalists in the military disasters of the rest of Judaism. He also rejected the revolutionary implications of Christianity. Taxes are to be paid. The civil authorities are the agents of God and obedience to them is a moral duty (Rom. 13.5f). Wives obey your husbands; slaves, your masters. The Mosaic law (which had immense prestige) is recognized to be just, holy, and spiritual (Rom. 7.12ff)—but it need not be observed, especially not the food laws and circumcision, which did so much to hinder the growth of Judaism and to isolate the Jews as a peculiar people (a dangerous social position). Rejection of the law leaves the believer free, and freedom was highly valued in a world much influenced by the Stoics and the cynics. But Paul's liberty is guided by the spirit and by common sense ("nature itself," I Cor. 11.14), and they both teach industry, thrift, obedience, good citizenship, moral propriety, and all those other homely virtues necessary for an individual to succeed in society, and for a small society—a local church—to succeed in the larger world. What early Christianity was like in the areas from which no material has been preserved can be inferred from the things Paul opposes in his letters, and this explains why no material has been preserved.

In spite of all this, the Christianity that became dominant in the second century took a positon somewhat to the legalist side of Paul. This appears most clearly in the question of baptism, and can now be explained from our understanding of "the mystery of the kingdom." Recent scholarship has shown that Paul's theory of baptism almost disappears from the works of second-century Christian writers of the party which ultimately proved triumphant (i.e., "orthodox"). These writers consistently represent the gift of the spirit as a promise of future life—not a present spiritual power and source of moral behavior, but a vague deposit to be protected by moral behavior. Notions of new birth, illumination, and exorcism occur, but are comparatively unimportant. The essential Pauline theme of death and resurrection with Christ is totally absent. These facts are not due to misunderstanding of Paul; in this connection there are no reminiscences of his works at all. Hence some scholars have supposed that "orthodox" second-century Christianity came largely from non-Pauline circles and that Paul was most venerated by the "heretics."

But this will not do. The great majority of the preserved works of early Christian literature, right through the second century, show clear Pauline influence. In particular, Pauline material is predominant in the New Testament, and the New Testament is the product of partisan selection—it shows which works the victorious party chose to accept as authoritative. So, to a lesser degree, does the later Christian material. Consequently the disappearance of Paul's theory of baptism during the second century cannot be explained by ignorance. It must have resulted from deliberate rejection. But if Paul represented safe, sane, and successful Christianity, and if this is why Pauline material predominates in the New Testament and in most of early Christian literature, why did the "orthodox" writers of the second century drop his doctrine of baptism?

The answer is that his doctrine of baptism was—with that of the eucharist—the most primitive and libertine element of his teaching. In other matters, secondary to the central Christian message, he had been more original and had worked out a safe compromise between the competing extremes. But for baptism he had substantially preserved and developed the teaching of Jesus. As the potentialities of this teaching became apparent, the socially and morally conservative found it unsafe. The libertines found in it all they needed: identification with Jesus, possession by his spirit, ascent into the heavens in his ascension, and consequent liberation from the law. Accordingly the gnostic teachers, many of whom emerged from the libertine tradition, made great use of Paul, but the "orthodox" shunned this side of his teaching until the persecutions of the third century and their own political triumph in the fourth had practically put an end to the libertine and gnostic parties.

The relation between the primitive secret tradition and gnosticism can be seen clearly in the case of Carpocrates, the founder of the sect attacked by Clement's letter.

Carpocrates is commonly thought to have worked in Alexandria during the years about A.D. 125. One of his followers was teaching in Rome, with considerable success, shortly after 150. References to his sect begin about 160, but the earliest are dubious and contain little information. Most of our knowledge about him and his followers comes from Clement and from Irenaeus of Lyons, another Church father who also wrote in the last decades of the second century.

Irenaeus gives an account of Carpocrates' teaching. Carpocrates believed that Jesus was the son of Joseph and was brought up in Judaism, realized the inadequacy of the Jewish law, turned to higher truths, and so received a supernatural power by which he was enabled to rise above the angels who had created this world, purging himself of his worldly passions as he went, and ascend to the supreme god. From this creed Carpocrates drew the conclusion that other men who achieved a similar contempt of human laws would be rewarded with equal or even greater powers, and he himself claimed to be able to dominate the angels and to use them for magical operations. These he did not hesitate to practice since he thought men were saved by faith and love alone. All other things were indifferent and were called good or bad only by human opinion. For this belief he, or at least his followers, appealed to a secret teaching of Jesus preserved in their sectarian books. On the other hand he (or they) also taught that souls are imprisoned in bodies and must pass from one body to another until they have performed all possible actions; only then will they have paid off their debt to the angels who created this world and will therefore be granted release from it. For this belief they found a scriptural basis in Lk. 12.58 and Mt. 5.25f. How (and whether) these beliefs were reconciled, Irenaeus does not say. He reports some interesting details: the Carpocratians brand their disciples on the backs of their right ears; they call themselves gnostics; they have pictures and images of Jesus (which they say derive from a picture of him made at the order of Pilate); these they crown with wreaths and set them up together with images of the philosophers —Pythagoras and Plato and Aristotle—and honor them all as the gentiles do (presumably, by burning incense before them). From Irenaeus' arguments against them it appears that they had considerable fame as miracle workers, denied the resurrection of the body, and practiced (or were accused of) extreme libertinism, especially in sexual relations. Irenaeus of course contrasts their miracles, as works of demons and of magic, with those of the Christians, as works of the holy spirit.

Irenaeus' account contains a good many apparently Platonic traits and Carpocrates' teaching has therefore been thought to come mainly from Platonism. But the Platonic traits are superficial and it is not surprising that libertine Christianity should have been superficially Platonized in Alexandria, as was "orthodox" Christianity (by Clement) and "normative" Judaism (by Philo). The fundamental structure—gift of the spirit, ascent to God, freedom from the law, and magical powers—is that found in the secret teaching of Jesus. The description of servitude to the cosmic powers, imprisonment in the body, transmigration from body to body, and

ultimate deliverance by undergoing all possible experiences, is obviously incompatible with that of ascent and immediate deliverance. The former was probably the Carpocratians' account of the
servitude of the average man, from which their own knowledge
of the secret way of salvation had set them free. It is clearly
Platonic, but evidently a secondary element in the structure, an
element Irenaeus made much of because of its potentialities for
scandal and for refutation.

From Clement I learned surprisingly little about Carpocrates.
He says that Carpocrates' son, Epiphanes, was the founder of "the
monadic gnosis" and of the Carpocratian sect, but both of these
statements are misrepresentative—the sect came, in fact, from
Carpocrates, as can be seen from Clement's published works as
well as from the new letter, and the monadic gnosis was based on
an early apocryphal work. Clement quotes some fragments of
Epiphanes' work justifying free love and communism by represent-
ing the world as the work of an egalitarian god. How (and
whether) these were reconciled with the theory of creation by
angels is uncertain; the creator angels may have followed a divine
plan. It appears that the sect celebrated orgiastic communion meals
which they said gave them access to the kingdom of God. Their
libertinism and indifferentism were justified by sayings of Jesus and
of Paul (or, agrapha quoted also by Paul?). Baptism played an important role in their theory, as did the notion of a new covenant,
but Clement's passing allusions do not permit a more precise account.

From both Cement and Irenaeus it is clear that the Carpocratians
were one of the most important of the gnostic sects. Irenaeus says
that Basilides and Carpocrates provided the starting points for all
the libertine sects, and in his refutations he puts the Carpocratians
second only to the Valentinians. Clement, when treating of libertine heretics, speaks of the Carpocratians first and discusses them at
far greater length than any of the others. After the time of

Clement and Irenaeus the sect seems to have dwindled rapidly. Less than half a century after Clement, Origen said he had never been able to meet a Carpocratian, and he may perhaps have been telling the truth. More important is the fact that almost none of the later writers against heretics add anything substantial to the information found in Irenaeus or Clement, or show any first-hand knowledge of the sect. Traditions about it lived on at least into fourth-century Palestine, and occasional statements in the later literature, like "Harpocrates used to cast out devils," may possibly be true.

From all this it appears that Carpocratian "gnosticism" was merely a Platonizing development of the primitive secret doctrine and practice of Jesus himself. Other gnostic groups certainly developed Christian doctrine with other elements (often bizarre), and some such groups may have been based on other aspects of Christian teaching, or on wholly non-Christian material. But it seems likely that the primitive secret tradition of Christianity will prove the most important single factor in solving one of the major problems of the history of gnosticism: Why did so very many gnostic sects spring up so early in so many parts of the Christian Church? Groups that seem gnostic occasionally appear in paganism or Judaism, but nowhere else is there anything like the quanity and vigor of the Christian development. This has to be explained, and the explanation must be something in Christianity. What else but the secret tradition?

That tradition, as followed in the present chapter, lay behind the resurrection visions, the ascension story, the coming of the spirit as a group phenomenon and its identification as the spirit of Jesus, the Jewish persecution of early Christianity, the conflict between the original apostles and James, the change in the character of the Jerusalem church and in its relation to Pharisaism after James' victory, the spread of libertine teachers through the early churches and of the polemic against them through the books of the New Testament, the "loss" of all writings from Jesus and his immediate disciples, the neglect of Paul's baptismal doctrine by the "orthodox" during the second century, and the early and widespread development of gnosticism in Christianity. That one theory should fit so many situations and explain so many problems of early Christianity is surprising and inclines me to think the theory may be correct. At all events, it is one possible solution of the major problem raised by Clement's Gospel—the nature and content of the secret tradition in early Christianity.

14

The History of the Document

While finishing the first draft of the report on my research, I made a study of the textual problems raised by the secret Gospel. The questions were: Was there any evidence, apart from Clement's letter, for the existence of the secret Gospel? How did the Gospel disappear and why do we never hear of it? When did Clement write his letter and what became of it after he had written it? How and when did it get to Mar Saba? What became of the manuscript from which the present text must have been copied? For these questions (excepting the first) there was almost no evidence. It was easy to find plausible answers, but impossible to prove them. I did what I could, and had the answers ready, so when I finally worked out the content and course of the libertine tradition I was at last able to give, at least in outline, an account of the secret Gospel down to the moment I set eyes on it. Much of the account is admittedly conjectural, as most historical explanations necessarily are. All I can claim for the following conjectures is that (1) they are not inherently improbable, and (2) they fit the facts already presented. So here is the account, from beginning to end:

The beginning of the Gospel was the coming of John the Baptist, who claimed to be a prophet sent by God to institute a new kind of immersion, one that would wash away sins. Among the crowds that went to him for this new baptism was Jesus. When

Jesus was baptized he felt himself possessed by a spirit and made a supernatural being, a "son of god," as the angels were said to be.

At that time there were already magical techniques being practiced in Palestine to give men the illusion of ascending into the heavens and receiving supernatural powers. Jesus may have been preconditioned for his baptismal experience by experimentation with such techniques, or he may have learned them after it. "Instinct"—something equally inexplicable and undeniable—plays a large part in self-hypnosis and in the development of the ability to hypnotize others, and Jesus evidently had unusual "instinctive" powers of suggestion. These powers enabled him to make a name for himself as an exorcist in Galilee, and to attract a circle of devoted followers. He of course tried to understand himself in the terms made available by his own culture, and seems to have thought himself, at first, a prophet, later, the Messiah. He also thought that he had ascended into the heavens, entered the kingdom of God, and was therefore freed from the Mosaic law.

A peculiar feature of the ancient techniques for "ascent" was that they provided for the initiation of others—the magician could take a pupil along on his "trip." Jesus therefore developed the Baptist's rite by adding to it an ascent into the kingdom, which gave his followers supernatural powers like his own and freed them, too, from the law. Finally, he added another rite, derived from ancient erotic magic, by which his followers were enabled, they believed, to eat his body and drink his blood and be joined with him, not only because possessed by his spirit, but also in physical union.

By use of these rites Jesus made himself the center of a libertine circle. After his crucifixion, his followers' emotional dependence on him and their previous hallucinations combined to make them see him risen from the dead. Next came sessions in which groups of them were seized by his spirit and expressed themselves by inarticulate utterance. These phenomena proved contagious and a large following was attracted. The new converts swelled an outer circle of followers which had aready existed in Jesus' time—those whom he had not chosen for entrance into the kingdom and who were therefore still under the law, though, perhaps, with some modifications. In Jerusalem, this outer circle found a leader in James, one of Jesus' brothers, who had not joined the movement during Jesus' lifetime but had come in after the crucifixion for reasons now uncertain—quite possibly prudential.

The Jewish groups most concerned about strict observance of the law—particularly the Pharisees and Sadducees—were aware of the libertine core of the Christian movement and therefore persecuted it. Finally, when Palestine was briefly given as a kingdom to Herod Agrippa I (A.D. 41–44), a friend of the Pharisees, Peter, the leader of Jesus' inner circle, was run out of Jerusalem; the other members of the inner circle also disappeared, and James was left in control. From then on the Jerusalem community adopted a policy of at least apparent observance of the law, relations with the Pharisees markedly improved, and there developed a party of strong observants who stood even to the right of James.

Jesus' libertine message and practice were carried to both Jews and gentiles outside Palestine by the original disciples, after they were driven out of Jerusalem, and also by later converts, some of whom had received the full initiation or believed themselves to have had equivalent experiences. Among these latter was Paul. From Paul's letters, written about A.D. 50, we can see the beginnings of a widespread and various libertine movement, by relation to which Paul occupied a mediating, comparatively conservative position.

Of the parties thus differentiated, the observant wing, centered in Jerusalem, never had much appeal outside Palestine and was hard hit in Palestine by the great Jewish revolts of 66–73 and 132–135. Thereafter its members were few and comparatively unimportant. The center, represented not only by Paul but also by many of the observant who were willing to compromise, gradually coalesced and gave rise, by the middle of the third century, to a clear majority that claimed to be "orthodox." The libertine wing gave rise to many of the gnostic heresies, but also persisted in esoteric groups, like that of Clement, within the "orthodox" communities.

It was probably the libertine wing that both produced and preserved the secret Gospel of Mark—a version of our canonical Mark expanded by the addition of material from the original, libertine tradition. Both the secret and the canonical Gospels were soon attributed to "Mark, the companion of Peter," who was already connected with Egypt by stories current in the thirties of the second century. Egypt was probably the place where the secret, expanded form of Mark originated, as other expansions, one observant (Matthew), one Pauline (Luke), originated in Syria and Asia Minor.

The material used in the secret text was drawn, at least in part, from an older Aramaic Gospel, a source used also by canonical Mark and by John. From this source, the Greek text of secret Mark was produced by a translation that was made after canonical Mark had been written (c. 75). The translator took canonical Mark as his model and imitated closely. His work seems to have been used by Matthew about A.D. 90. Luke may have known it, too; John did not. It evidently was used by Carpocrates in Egypt about 125. Traces of its influence appear in a form of the text of the canonical Gospels (the so-called "western text"), that originated in Egypt shortly before 150. Another trace of the secret Gospel probably appears in the work of a gnostic named Theodotus who wrote in Egypt during the 160's: Clement quoted from him a report that Jesus taught the disciples, "at first by examples and by stories with hidden meanings, then by parables and by enigmas, but in the third stage, clearly and nakedly, in private." Other parallels to the secret Gospel can be found in early Christian apocrypha—especially some of those from Egypt—and in a few of the early works of the Church fathers. Some of these parallels may indicate knowledge of the text, but most will have come from similar traditions.

After the letter of Clement, there is no clear evidence for the secret Gospel's existence. Its disappearance was probably due to the persecution that devastated Alexandrian Christianity about A.D. 200 or 210. Clement is commonly supposed to have been driven from the city at this time. Origen is said to have become head of the catechetical school at eighteen because there were no men left in the city. This is probably legend, but the legend at least indicates that the persecution was remembered as unusually severe. The Carpocratians in Alexandria may have been wiped out. Since the secret Gospel was probably represented by a few texts only—some, but hardly many, among the Carpocratians, one or two in the inner circle of Clement's church—it could easily have been lost at this time. Book burning was a standard feature of ancient religious persecutions.

After the destruction of the manuscripts of the secret Gospel, the only clear evidence of its existence was Clement's letter. This has so many parallels to the third book of his *Stromateis* that it most likely dates from the same time (190–200?). But this date is not certain—the parallels are largely due to the subject matter, and Clement may have long gone on saying the same things about the Carpocratians. Since the letter was found in Palestine, its recipient, Theodore, may have lived there. "Theodore" was a popular name among Christians of Jewish ancestry; it translates a number of common Hebrew names like Nathan, Jonathan, etc. Clement had studied in Palestine under a Christian teacher of Jewish ancestry, and he had a number of friends there. One of his warmest admirers, Alexander, afterward became bishop of Jerusalem and Clement dedicated to him a work against Judaizing heretics.

All this makes it likely that our letter was sent to Palestine. We know that a collection of Clement's letters did exist in the Monastery of Mar Saba during the eighth century. Three passages from them were quoted by a writer called John of Damascus, who worked there from 716 to 749. Since no trace of Clement's letters is found anywhere else, it seems probable that our letter did come from this collection. It certainly came from some collection; that is proved by its heading, "From the letters of Clement." John of Damascus cites a "twenty-first letter," so there must have been at least that many in his collection; probably there were more.

Perhaps the collection was made by Clement's friend, the bishop Alexander. He would have had many precedents; collections of letters of eminent Christians, beginning with those of Paul, had long been common. The fourth-century Church historian, Eusebius, said that the library in Jerusalem was rich in collections of letters which he had used for his history, but he knew nothing of a collection of Clement's letters. It may have been misplaced or mistitled or located in some minor church or private library that escaped his attention.

Alternatively, the collection may have been made elsewhere or at a later date. A later date is suggested by the heading which gives Clement some titles ("most holy," "author of the *Stromateis*") that appear only in later authors. But the heading is conventional and might be the work of any man who made or copied the excerpt, down to the writer of the present manuscript; it cannot be used to date the collection from which the excerpt was taken. And it is hard to find a later time at which Clement was so popular that anyone would want to collect his letters.

Clement's works were very rarely cited, copied, or forged. A cluster of citations comes from the late fifth, sixth, and seventh centuries, but if the letters had not been collected before then it is unlikely that any of them would have been left to collect. Early manuscripts of Clement are rare; for most of his main work there is only one. The rarity shows that he was not much thought of; had he been popular and influential more copies would have been made. Besides copying, another good indication of a Church father's popularity in the middle ages is the number of works forged in his name; in Clement's name there are only three and these are evidently late and isolated. There is no sign of any general interest in Clement at any time when the present text could have been forged. Even appeals to Clement as a doctrinal authority are comparatively rare. So it seems likely that the collection was made early and thereafter neglected.

That such a collection should have existed for centuries without being cited is not surprising, neither is the fact that the one writer who did cite it should have said nothing about the text of the secret Gospel. There are a number of examples of texts that have survived for a thousand years without being cited, and medieval authors—especially monks—were often unwilling to quote or even to refer to material they thought possibly heretical. There is a long list of ancient secret Gospels of which we know little more than the names because the Church fathers did not choose to preserve— or chose to destroy—the content. One Syrian bishop boasts of having destroyed more than two hundred copies of a Gospel made by piecing together the four canonical ones. The editor had been a heretic; that was enough.

Consequently lack of reference to the letter of Clement is no argument against its authenticity. Indeed, the lack of reference is easier to explain if the letter is genuine. If genuine, it was, to begin with, a private and confidential letter. No mention of it was to be expected in the years immediately after it was written, say from 200 to 225. But the Carpocratians are said to have become rare and insignificant by about 225, and once they had become unimportant the letter would interest no one but a historian. Historians were rare in the medieval Church, and historians willing to report unorthodox traditions from the early fathers were very rare. So the lack of reference to the letter would be explicable. But if the letter was a forgery it must have been written and attributed to Clement for some purpose of propaganda; it must have been intended to be circulated and to attract attention. If so, the fact that no reference to it has been preserved would be harder to explain. So the total neglect of the letter through seventeen centuries argues for its authenticity. The monks of Mar Saba wrote no histories of the early Church; their literary productions were hymns, works on prayer, fasting, and church discipline, and lives of martyrs.

There is no telling when the collection containing the letter got into the library at Mar Saba. The monastery was founded in the late fifth century, and any date from then on to the seventeenth century is possible. Even the citations by John of Damascus do not absolutely prove that the source of our manuscript was already there—they may have been taken from a different collection. The likelihood, though, is that the collection then used was the one from which the present excerpt was made, and that this collection remained in Mar Saba down to the eighteenth century.

The life of the monastery seems to have been continuous—or practically continuous—during all that time. The buildings were occasionally pillaged or even "destroyed," but the monks seem never to have been driven away for long, and some of their manuscripts may have survived. The original settlement was a collection of caves in two cliffs; later these were enlarged and given stone facings, and some stone buildings were constructed on terraces in front of them. There was little in the complex to burn; manuscripts in the caves were not likely to be taken as loot by bedouin; some have actually been found in abandoned caves. Reportedly when attacks seemed imminent the most important manuscripts were hidden in nearby caves outside the monastery. These reports seem plausible because the Qumran community, at the end of the canyon in which the monastery stands, already followed this practice.

Thus the manuscript collection of Clement's letters may have stayed at Mar Saba from the fifth century to the eighteenth, perhaps being copied once or twice during the period. On the other hand, it may have migrated half a dozen times from one monastery to another in southern Palestine. Many texts did so. The strongest reason for thinking this one remained at Mar Saba is that it was found there. Another reason is the fact that nobody referred to it. This suggests that it did not circulate, but lay neglected in some corner of a single library.

Whatever its previous history, most of the collection of Clement's letters probably perished in the great fire which burned out the treasury of Mar Saba in the early years of the eighteenth century. The treasury was a cave in which many of the oldest manuscripts and other antiquities of the monastery had been stored. Air supply to this cave is limited and present monastic tradition says that the fire smouldered for two weeks before the monks could get through the smoke to put it out. Books are hard to burn, at best; they usually char around the edges and then go out. So after this fire there were probably a great many loose manuscript leaves, almost undamaged, salvaged from the unburned centers of old manuscripts. Over a century later the remains of the Mar Saba manuscripts were carried off to Jerusalem. The man who (yet later) catalogued the Jerusalem collection remarked on the great number of isolated leaves from old manuscripts which had gone to pieces. Many such isolated leaves are still to be found both in Jerusalem and at Mar Saba where lots of them have been used for bookbinding.

The fragmentary state of the present letter should probably be explained by supposing it a copy of such an isolated leaf. There was much copying of old manuscripts at Mar Saba in the seventeenth and eighteenth centuries. Somebody's attention was caught by the surprising content of this leaf. He studied the text, corrected it as best he could, and then copied it into the back of the monastery's edition of the letters of Ignatius of Antioch, since it resembled them in being a letter from an early father attacking gnostic heretics. There are lots of examples of late copyists correcting their texts—sometimes none too well. But this man seems to have done a good job. The very few mistakes in the present text are doubtless due to his haste while making this copy, probably a little after 1750.

All this history is merely plausible, and plausibility is not proof. Things probably happened thus, though they may have happened otherwise. History, however, is by definition the search for the *most probable* explanations of preserved phenomena. When several explanations are possible, the historian must always choose the most probable one. But the truth is that improbable things sometimes happen. Therefore truth is necessarily stranger than history.

THE END

Postscript

For this reprinting the editor asked me to write a short account of how the new document and my books on it[1] have been received.

Briefly, there was an initial flash of publicity, with newspaper and journal reports all over the world, then came a swarm of attacks in religious periodicals, assuring their readers that the new material was unimportant and my theories about it "venal popularization," as one Jesuit wrote,[2] or, in the words of another, "a morbid concatenation of fancies."[3] Protestant fundamentalists were no less abusive, and even the old Episcopal clergyman whom *The New York Times,* in its wisdom, asked to review this volume, felt compelled to conclude his sermonette with an exhortation, "But, dear reader, do not be alarmed," Christianity is *"true"* (his italics).[4] Why those who worship Jesus should think further information about him "alarming" is an interesting question.

---

1. *The Secret Gospel* and *Clement of Alexandria and a Secret Gospel of Mark,* Harvard University Press, Cambridge, Mass., 1973. Henceforth *"Clement."* It presented the Greek text of Clement's letter, a detailed commentary, and the arguments and evidence for the conclusions that *The Secret Gospel* summarizes.

2. *For works not identified in the notes, see the bibliography at the end of this Postscript.* Those listed there are cited here by the authors' names alone. This is Fitzmyer, p. 572. Fitzmyer knew *Clement* (he discussed it in this review) so he must have known that *The Secret Gospel* was an attempt to make the results of years of research accessible to the average reader, *not* something invented for popular appeal. His representation of it as the latter would therefore seem to have been deliberately false. His article was full of similar falsities, but they are not worth discussion, nor is he.

3. Skehan, p. 452.

4. Parker, *N.Y. Times Book Review,* p. 5.

Fortunately there were also favorable reviews. H. Trevor-Roper, Regius Professor of History at Oxford, wrote an enthusiastic one in the London *Sunday Times.* Helmut Koester, Professor of New Testament at Harvard, wrote in *The American Historical Review,* "No student of the New Testament and of the history of early Christianity can afford to neglect the significance of the new text published here, nor . . . the issues this book raises and debates on the basis of unparalleled knowledge of such a variety of relevant source materials."[5] Similarly, E. Trocmé, Professor of New Testament at the University of Strasbourg, although he disagreed with some of my interpretations, wrote of the work as a whole, "L'ouvrage de M. Smith est un monument d'érudition et un modèle d'argumentation critique. . . . Il doit être salué comme un très grand livre."[6] I value his judgment particularly because of our disagreement.

Some of the reviews began the scholarly discussion. It has continued mainly in articles in professional journals of New Testament criticism, and has gone slowly, since the problems raised by the text are complex and the relevant evidence is extensive. I should guess that in the nine years after the books' appearance about 200 or 250 printed items of all kinds, from newspaper reports to pamphlets, have dealt with the new material. Of these I have seen about 150, from which those listed in the bibliography seem to me the most significant. "Significant" is a deliberately vague word; I have included a few I think worthless but influential.[7]

5. Koester, *The American Historical Review,* p. 622. "This book" refers to *Clement,* but the comments apply equally to *The Secret Gospel.*

6. Trocmé, p. 292. "The work of M. Smith is a monument of erudition and a model of critical argument. . . . It should be recognized as a very great book." This also referred particularly to *Clement.*

7. For example, Achtemeier's review, of which the pretendedly factual statements are often grossly inaccurate. Though worthless as criticism, it cannot confidently be described as "useless." It probably pleased Fitzmyer, who was then editor of *The Journal of Biblical Literature,* and thus may have helped Achtemeier get the secretaryship of the Society of Biblical Literature. That both names rhyme with "liar" is a curious coincidence.

Since point by point discussion of these articles would take much space, I shall indicate briefly the main questions and the range of critical opinions about each.

First, is the letter by Clement of Alexandria? The great majority of critics agree that it is, though a minority have hedged their opinions ("as a working hypothesis," etc.) or have left the question unanswered. Only four have come out against the attribution,[8] and nobody has produced any strong argument to prove Clement could *not* have written it. Since the evidence from style and content, indicating that that he *did* write it, is extremely strong, there seems little point in discussing more or less groundless conjectures as to how or why somebody else *might possibly* have written it. Only if a strong argument can be made against Clement's authorship will the question have to be reconsidered. So long as no such case is forthcoming, the matter can be taken as settled.

This settles also the *latest possible* date for the secret gospel. Since Clement describes it as a treasured heirloom of his church, it must have been there at least a generation before his time, i.e., by about 150. (He wrote about 175 to 200, and was not the sort of man to make up such a claim out of whole cloth.) If he is right in saying it was used by Carpocrates, who flourished about 125, it would have to be somewhat earlier than Carpocrates' time. This would push it back into the neighborhood of the canonical gospels which are commonly dated between 70 and 100. Consequently the next important question is that of its relation to them.

My conclusion from its style, that the writer imitated canonical Mark and therefore was later, has generally been accepted. If canonical Mark is to be dated about 75, the *earliest possible* date for the present text of the secret gospel would be sometime in the 80s. But what sources did the author use, and how is his work

8. Kümmel, Murgia, Musurillo, Quesnell. Quesnell's absurd insinuation that I forged the whole thing has been generally received with the contempt it deserved. In my reply (cited in the bibliography, under Quesnell) I disproved the evidence he pretended to have found, but this was hardly necessary.

related to the other canonical gospels? The reader will remember that the evidence about these points seemed contradictory and that I tried to explain it by several theories which can be simplified to the following: An original Aramaic gospel (about A.D. 50?) was twice translated into Greek. Canonical Mark (about 75?) used one translation, John (about 100?) another. Though each left out some elements and added many, their use of different versions of this common source accounts for their similarities of outline and differences of wording. Canonical Mark was then reworked at least four times—by the author of secret Mark, by Matthew, by Luke, and by the Carpocratians (who are said to have used secret Mark).

About this theory and the facts it tries to explain there has been much dispute. Nobody wholly agrees with anybody else (this is usual in New Testament studies), but the critics do drift into two main groups. The larger group thinks secret Mark was made up from bits of the canonical gospels which the author put together and expanded by his own inventions; the smaller group thinks it was based at least in part on pre-Markan traditions.[9] Whether such traditions were oral or written, and, if written, whether in leaflets containing only one or two episodes, or in some sort of coherent composition (a collection of miracle stories? or a gospel?)—these are questions still open.

Scholars who hold the majority view of secret Mark's origins do not have to ask what it tells us about Jesus—this is one of the main reasons for the view's popularity, in spite of its failure to explain secret Mark's relation to John. If declared a pastiche it can be dismissed as a product of some second century church, informative

9. Smaller—not by much. Of the authors in the bibliography who have discussed this question, 11 find evidence of pre-Markan tradition (Beardslee, Donfried, Fuller, Frend (?), Johnson, Kee, Koester, MacRae, Pedersen, Trocme (?), Wink), 15 find none (Brown, Bruce, Fitzmyer, Grant, Hanson (?), Hobbs, van der Horst, Kümmel, Merkel, Mullins, Parker, Richardson, Schmidt, Shepherd, Skehan).

only about that church's interests and inventiveness. Since none of these scholars has any good evidence as to what church this could have been, their theories—like most theories about the background (*Sitz im Leben*) of gospel stories—leave the story seated nowhere, but floating free in warm air.

The large minority, however, who agree that secret Mark somehow preserves pre-Markan traditions, have to face the question about the reliability of those traditions, especially that about the nocturnal initiation. Why the specified costume, the sheet over the naked body? What was "the mystery of the kingdom of God"? Any attempt to answer such questions, i.e., to explain what ancient authors deliberately concealed, must be conjectural, and many scholars reject on principle all conjectures except their own. Consequently I expected that mine about these problems would be generally rejected, the more so because they introduced notions unfashionable (Jesus practiced baptism) or shocking (and magic!). I was not disappointed. But I was much surprised by the number of scholars who were willing to concede that Jesus might have had some secret doctrines or initiatory ceremonies,[10] and of those who would recognize, even if unwillingly and with many reservations, that magic did have a role in the first century Church.[11]

Much of the unwillingness to go further was due, I think, to unfamiliarity with the terrain. No one was well acquainted with the outsiders' traditions about Jesus, nor (at that time) with the texts from ancient magic and their similarities to the gospels. Lacking familiarity with this source material, most critics could not see the grounds for many of the historical judgments made or implied in my arguments. It is significant that most of the group

10. Betz, Johnson, Koester, Grant, van der Horst.
11. Bruce, Frend, Betz, Koester, Grant, van der Horst, Richardson, Trevor-Roper, Wink.

prepared to go along part way were those who had most knowledge of comparable pagan material. From all this it was clear that the data about Jesus and magic had to be much more fully collected and put together in a clear historical structure. This I tried to do in *Jesus the Magician*.[12]

12. Harper and Row, San Francisco, 1978; to be republished by them in paperback in 1982.

Bibliography

P. Achtemeier, review, *Journal of Biblical Literature* 93 (1974) 625–28.

W. Beardslee, review, *Interpretation* 28 (1974) 234–36.

H. D. Betz, response to Fuller, see Fuller.

R. Brown, "The Relation of 'The Secret Gospel of Mark' to the Fourth Gospel," *Catholic Biblical Quarterly* 36 (1974) 466–85.

F. Bruce, *The 'Secret' Gospel of Mark* (E. Wood Lecture 1974) London: Athlone Press, 1974.

K. Donfried, "New-Found Fragments of an Early Gospel," *Christian Century* 90 (1973) 759–60.

J. Fitzmyer, "How to Exploit a Secret Gospel," *America* 128 (1973) 570–72. See my reply and his, printed by the editors of *America* under the title, "Mark's 'Secret Gospel'?" 129 (1973) 64–65.

W. Frend, "A New Jesus?" *New York Review of Books* 20 (1973) 34–35.

R. Fuller, *Longer Mark: Forgery, Interpolation, or Old Tradition?* (Center for Hermeneutical Studies, Colloquy 18) ed. W. Wuellner; Berkeley: Center for Hermeneutical Studies, 1975. This contains

155

156

responses by a dozen scholars, of which some are mere notes, but the following deserve notice: H. D. Betz 17–18, E. Hobbs 19–25, S. Johnson 26–28, H. Koester 29–32, A. Kolenkow 33–34, C. Murgia 35–40, D. Schmidt 41–45, M. Shepherd 46–52, M. Smith 12–15.

R. Grant, "Morton Smith's Two Books," *Anglican Theological Review* 56 (1974) 58–65.

R. Hanson, review, *Journal of Theological Studies* 25 (1974) 513–21.

E. Hobbs, response to Fuller, see Fuller.

P. van der Horst, "Het 'Geheime Markusevangelie,'" *Nederlands Theologisch Tijdschrift* 33 (1979) 27–51.

S. Johnson, "The Mystery of St. Mark," *History Today* 25 (1975) 89–97.

——— , response to Fuller, see Fuller.

H. Kee, review, *Journal of the American Academy of Religion* 43 (1975) 326–29.

H. Koester, review, *American Historical Review* 80 (1975) 620–22.

——— , response to Fuller, see Fuller.

A. Kolenkow, response to Fuller, see Fuller.

W. Kümmel, "Ein Jahrzent Jesusforschung (1965–1975)," *Theologische Rundschau* NF 40 (1975) 298–303.

G. MacRae, "Yet Another Jesus," *Commonweal* 99 (1974) 417–20.

H. Merkel, "Auf den Spuren des Urmarkus?" *Zeitschrift fuer Theologie und Kirche* 71 (1974) 123–44. See my reply, "Merkel on the Longer Text of Mark," ibid. 72 (1975) 133–50.

T. Mullins, "Papias and Clement and Mark's Two Gospels," *Vigiliae Christianae* 30 (1976) 189–92.

C. Murgia, response to Fuller, see Fuller.

H. Musurillo, "Morton Smith's Secret Gospel," *Thought* 48 (1974) 327–31.

P. Parker, "An early Christian cover-up?" *New York Times Book Review*, July 22, 1973, 5.

————, "On Professor Morton Smith's Find at Mar Saba," *Anglican Theological Review* 56 (1974) 53–57.

N. Petersen, review, *Southern Humanities Review* 8 (1974) 525–31.

M. Pomilio, "Il frammento di Mar Saba Un Vangelo Segreto?" *Studi Cattolici* 21 (1978) 10–16.

Q. Quesnell, "The Mar Saba Clementine: A Question of Evidence," *Catholic Biblical Quarterly* 37 (1975) 48–67. See my reply, "On the Authenticity of the Mar Saba Letter of Clement," ibid. 38 (1976) 196–99, and Quesnell's "A Reply to Morton Smith," ibid., 200–203.

J. Reese, review, *Catholic Biblical Quarterly* 36 (1974) 434–35.

C. Richardson, review, *Theological Studies* 35 (1974) 571–77.

D. Schmidt, response to Fuller, see Fuller.

M. Shepherd, response to Fuller, see Fuller.

P. Skehan, review, *Catholic Historical Review* 60 (1974) 451–53.

M. Smith, responses, see Fitzmyer, Fuller, Merkel, Quesnell.

H. Trevor-Roper, "Gospel of Liberty," (London) *Sunday Times,* June 30, 1974, 15.

E. Trocmé, "Trois critiques au miroir de l'évangile selon Marc," *Revue d'histoire et de philosophie religieuses* 55 (1975) 289–95.

W. Wink, "Jesus as Magician," *Union Seminary Quarterly Review* 30 (1974) 3–14.

A Call for the Radical Reformation of Christianity

by Da Free John

A Call for the
Radical Reformation
of Christianity

Da Free John

The greatest spiritual figures of history, the God-Realized Adepts, have always purified the religious traditions of their times. In this booklet of excerpts from a forthcoming text, Da Free John praises the radical Spirituality Taught by Jesus and reveals the errors of conventional Christianity—its ego-based illusion of vicarious salvation without personal self-sacrifice, and its provincial belief that Jesus is the only source of Divine Help in the world.

"Jesus was a radical Teacher. He instructed people within his native tradition, but he Taught them how to transcend themselves and their religious conventionality via a direct and radical process of God-Communion."

"The Great Adepts are born to Help mankind to Realize the Truth—not, like pharisees and other conventional religionists, to prevent themselves as well as all others from the Realization of Divine or Transcendental Bliss and Love. Therefore, it is time for Christians to finish the Reformation and resort to the Teaching and the God of Jesus. Christians must renounce 'Caesar's' priests and State religions. Christians must surrender themselves, one by one, to the Living Spiritual and Transcendental God, and so enter the Great Way nakedly, free of all self-armor, superiority, moral righteousness, and conflict with other lovers of Truth."

—Da Free John

38 pages, $2.00

Available by mail order—see last page of this section for ordering information.

ALSO FROM THE DAWN HORSE PRESS

THE BOOKS OF MASTER DA FREE JOHN

SOURCE TEXTS

THE KNEE OF LISTENING
The Early Life and Radical Spiritual Teachings of
Bubba [Da] Free John
$6.95 paper

THE METHOD OF THE SIDDHAS
Talks with Bubba [Da] Free John on the Spiritual Technique of the Saviors of
Mankind
$12.95 paper

THE HYMN OF THE MASTER
A Confessional Recitation on the Mystery of the Spiritual Master based on the
principal verses of the Guru Gita *(freely selected, rendered, and adapted)*
$8.95 paper

THE FOUR FUNDAMENTAL QUESTIONS
Talks and essays about human experience and the actual practice of an
Enlightened Way of Life
$1.95 paper

THE LIBERATOR (ELEUTHERIOS)
A summation of the "radical process" of Enlightenment, or God-Realization,
taught by the "Western Adept," Master Da Free John
$12.95 cloth, $6.95 paper

THE ENLIGHTENMENT OF THE WHOLE BODY
A Rational and New Prophetic Revelation of the Truth of Religion, Esoteric
Spirituality, and the Divine Destiny of Man
$18.95 paper

SCIENTIFIC PROOF OF THE EXISTENCE OF GOD WILL SOON BE
ANNOUNCED BY THE WHITE HOUSE!
Prophetic Wisdom about the Myths and Idols of mass culture and popular
religious cultism, the new priesthood of scientific and political materialism, and
the secrets of Enlightenment hidden in the body of Man
$12.95 paper

THE PARADOX OF INSTRUCTION
An Introduction to the Esoteric Spiritual Teaching of Bubba [Da] Free John
$14.95 cloth

NIRVANASARA
Radical Transcendentalism and the Introduction of Advaitayana Buddhism
$9.95 paper

MANUALS OF PRACTICE

COMPULSORY DANCING
Talks and Essays on the spiritual and evolutionary necessity of emotional surrender to the Life-Principle
$2.95 paper

THE WAY THAT I TEACH
Talks on the Intuition of Eternal Life
$14.95 cloth, $12.95 paper

THE YOGA OF CONSIDERATION AND
THE WAY THAT I TEACH
Talks and essays on the distinction between preliminary practices and the radical Way of prior Enlightenment
$8.95 paper

THE BODILY SACRIFICE OF ATTENTION
Introductory Talks on Radical Understanding and the Life of Divine Ignorance
$12.95 paper

"I" IS THE BODY OF LIFE
Talks and Essays on the Art and Science of Equanimity and the Self-Transcending Process of Radical Understanding
$12.95 paper

THE BODILY LOCATION OF HAPPINESS
On the Incarnation of the Divine Person and the Transmission of Love-Bliss
$8.95 paper

PRACTICAL TEXTS

CONSCIOUS EXERCISE AND THE TRANSCENDENTAL SUN
The principle of love applied to exercise and the method of common physical action. A science of whole body wisdom, or true emotion, intended most especially for those engaged in religious or spiritual life
$12.95 cloth

THE EATING GORILLA COMES IN PEACE
The Transcendental Principle of Life Applied to Diet and the Regenerative Discipline of True Health
$12.95 paper

RAW GORILLA
The Principles of Regenerative Raw Diet Applied in True Spiritual Practice
$3.95 paper

LOVE OF THE TWO-ARMED FORM
The Free and Regenerative Function of Sexuality in Ordinary Life, and the Transcendence of Sexuality in True Religious or Spiritual Practice
$12.95 paper

FOR CHILDREN

WHAT TO REMEMBER TO BE HAPPY
A Spiritual Way of Life for Your First Fourteen Years or So
$3.95 paper

I AM HAPPINESS
A Rendering for Children of the Spiritual Adventure of Master Da Free John Adapted by Daji Bodha and Lynne Closser from
The Knee of Listening *by Master Da Free John*
$9.95 paper

PERIODICALS

CRAZY WISDOM
The Monthly Journal of The Crazy Wisdom Fellowship
12 copies $25.00

THE LAUGHING MAN
The Alternative to Scientific Materialism and Religious Provincialism
4 copies (quarterly) $10.00

CLASSIC SPIRITUAL LITERATURE

THE YOGA OF LIGHT
The Classic Esoteric Handbook of Kundalini Yoga
by Hans-Ulrich Rieker,
translated by Elsy Becherer
$5.95 paper

A NEW APPROACH TO BUDDHISM
by Dhiravamsa
$2.95 paper

VEDANTA AND CHRISTIAN FAITH
by Bede Griffiths
$3.50 paper

FOUNDING THE LIFE DIVINE
by Morwenna Donnelly
$3.95 paper

BREATH, SLEEP, THE HEART, AND LIFE
The Revolutionary Health Yoga of Pundit Acharya
$5.95 paper

THE SPIRITUAL INSTRUCTIONS OF SAINT SERAPHIM OF SAROV
Edited and with an introduction by Da Free John
$3.50 paper

THE SONG OF THE SELF SUPREME
Astavakra Gita
Preface by Da Free John
Translated by Radhakamal Mukerjee
$8.95 paper

Publications from The Dawn Horse Press are available at fine bookstores or by mail order. To order by mail, please add to price shown postage and handling in the amount of $1.25 for first item, $.35 for each additional item. California residents add 6% sales tax. Address to:

THE DAWN HORSE BOOK DEPOT
P.O. Box 3680, Dept. SG
Clearlake, CA 95422